Sometimes you win Sometimes you learn

Terry O'Brien is a bestselling author, columnist, consultant and motivational trainer. He is highly sought after in the corporate as well as the academic world, and has been training managers and providing counselling and consultancy over the past couple of decades.

Author of hugely popular books on motivation, effective change and all that is 'un-Google-able,' his writings focus on skill development and communication techniques. Terry O'Brien is a firm believer that 'infotainment' is a must for content to be effective, and his books are all about the three Rs: Read, Record and Recall.

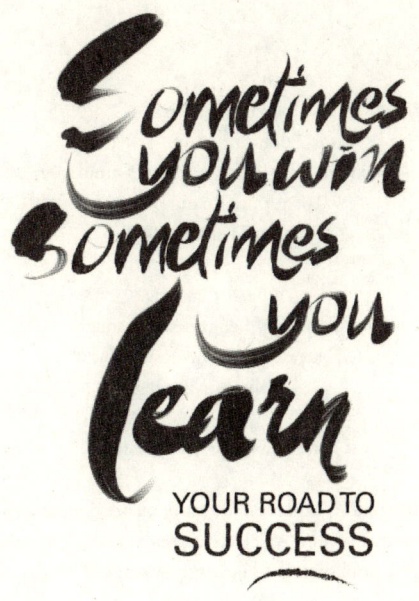

Sometimes you win Sometimes you learn

YOUR ROAD TO
SUCCESS

TERRY O'BRIEN

RUPA

Published by
Rupa Publications India Pvt. Ltd
in association with Pilar Outreach Foundation 2023
7/16, Ansari Road, Daryaganj
New Delhi 110002

Sales Centres:
Prayagraj Bengaluru Chennai
Hyderabad Jaipur Kathmandu
Kolkata Mumbai

Copyright © Terry O'Brien 2023

The views and opinions expressed in this book are the author's own and the
facts are as reported by him which have been verified to the extent possible,
and the publishers are not in any way liable for the same.

All rights reserved.
No part of this publication may be reproduced, transmitted,
or stored in a retrieval system, in any form or by any means, electronic,
mechanical, photocopying, recording or otherwise, without the prior
permission of the publisher.

P-ISBN: 978-93-5702-308-5
E-ISBN: 978-93-5702-321-4

First impression 2023

10 9 8 7 6 5 4 3 2 1

Printed in India

This book is sold subject to the condition that it shall not, by way of
trade or otherwise, be lent, resold, hired out, or otherwise circulated,
without the publisher's prior consent, in any form of binding or
cover other than that in which it is published.

*This book is dedicated to the
Pilar Outreach Foundation, which motivates
people to empower themselves to follow their dreams.*

CONTENTS

Introduction ix
1. Road to the Destination 1
2. Attitude 26
3. The Power of Skills 55
4. Character Building 91
5. Self-Image 103
6. Motivational Snippets 114

INTRODUCTION

A 38-year-old civilian research pilot travelled 240,000 miles in 76 hours on 19 July 1969 and scripted history. He reached his destination. Yes, a man from planet Earth first set foot upon the moon. It was none other than Neil Armstrong. His prophetic words seemed to be written across the sky: *'That's one small step for man, one giant leap for mankind.'* He touched the moon, and in all probability, the moon smiled. This small step has indeed taken a quantum leap in space research at present. Today, we are moving towards space tourism. Now, we have SpaceX, which helps tourists to reach out into space. The world's first space tourist Dennis Tito, aged 82, wants a chance to relive the joy of his trip to the International Space Station (ISS), now that he has retired and has time on his hands. Tito longs to go back; only this time, he has signed up for a spin around the moon aboard Elon Musk's Starship.

From the laidback times of the 1950s and 60s, we now move ahead with race neck breakspeed; the road to our destination is fast changing with new speed. 'Slow and steady wins' is now an anachronism; this has given way to the new dynamic—fast and steady wins the race. However, the base canons of success remain the same.

The odds are there though. Early in March 1967, in Eastern Canada, an 11-year-old child died of old age. He was only 11 years old chronologically, but he suffered from an odd disease called Progeria—advanced aging—and he exhibited many characteristics of a 90-year-old man. In fact, he was an old man when he died—long lifetime of biological change packed into 11 short years.

Today, it is a fast-changing world, so the road to our destination has many more challenges. Young people today get burnt out in a short span of time. Burn out is a state of emotional, physical and mental exhaustion caused by excessive and prolonged stress. This happens at an early stage in one's life or career because they have achieved too much too quickly.

The rudiments remain the same—what is required is the right attitude and character and, of course, preparation to innovate in a social landscape where communication with a difference becomes the essence for making our presence felt. It is time to ponder over a 'small step' that in time will lead to a 'giant leap'. It is now or never—it's time to map out with direction to open our road to success, both as an individual and a professional. The bottom line is to have two kinds of victory—private victory and public victory.

If we don't start, it's certain we can't arrive. If your image improves, your performance improves. The balance is a must—the mind completes whatever picture we put in it. You must feel that you deserve success before success gets to you.

Opportunity for success lies within us all. You can get to the pinnacle of success by getting to the bottom of things.

Success is easy once you believe.

Happy road to your destination.

Yours truly,
Terry O'Brien

1

ROAD TO THE DESTINATION

Where were you born? Where is your home? Where are you going? What are you doing? Think about these once in a while and watch your answers change.

—RICHARD BACH

On the highway, I stopped to ask a man on the crossroads, 'Bro, where does this road lead to?' His simple answer gave me the first roadmap to success: 'That depends on where you want to go!'

The simplest questions are the most profound.

Destination is what matters; Destiny matters not. As we traverse the passage of time in life, we get to know that the journey is better than the destination and that learning the map of our progress is significant. Life is indeed a learning school! We may fail at times but that will not deter us from emerging successful when we understand FAIL. Fail to fail is also a process of learning. In fact, if we re-look at the word 'FAIL' as an acronym, we get the correct message, which is always positive—'First Attempt In Learning'. Butterflies are caterpillars that fight back and come off with flying colours. Just when the caterpillar thought that the world was over, it became a butterfly. Life has got all these twists and turns; there is no guarantee that one can find himself/herself in a win–win situation. Indeed, sometimes we win, sometimes we do not lose—we learn. Don't look down, look up. If you keep your face always towards the sunshine, the shadows will fall behind you. If one falls into a river, he will not drown; it is only when he remains there that will make him drown.

*Remember this: Nothing is written in the stars.
Not these stars, nor any others. No one controls your destiny.*

—GREGORY MAGUIRE

'It is hard work that can get you to where you are', said Napoléon.

When Napoléon was a young soldier, he visited a renowned palm reader to ask if he would ever become emperor. The palm reader told him dismissively that he didn't have a fate line. Napoléon drew his sword and gashed a deep line—a fate line—on his palm. He turned his bloodied hand to the palmist and asked, 'How about now?' Napoléon wasn't willing to compromise on his ambitions.

Determination and persistence pays off.[1]

---

[1] Swarup, Radhika, 'It Was Hard Work That Got Me to Where I Am, Not Fate', *Huffpost*, 21 June 2015, https://tinyurl.com/46s64rmw. Accessed on 30 April 2023.

Our destiny is not written for us, it's written by us.

—BARACK OBAMA

However, most people in the world believe their failures and successes are because of destiny. There is a well-known story of a man called Mr Jonah who was waiting at an airport to board a flight. While waiting, he tried the weighing machine, not so much for his weight as much as a line of fortune on the reverse side of the card. Jonah inserted the coin and out came the card which surprised him: *Your name is Jonah. You weigh 145 pounds. You are going to board the 4.20 flight to London.* Jonah presumed somebody was tracking him, a Sherlock Holmes perhaps! In order to double check, he tried the coin again and out came the card, *You are still Jonah. You still weigh 145 pounds and you are still going to take the 4.20 flight to London.* He was dismayed. He went into the men's washroom. He tried to camouflage his face and returned so that nobody recognizes his visage. Lo and behold, the card this time read, *You are still Jonah. You still weigh 145 pounds, but the flight you were supposed to take to London at 4.20 has left.* Most of us miss the flight as we look at destiny, not ourselves. The future is right there for us to grab. It is time to script success with our sweat and toil and perseverance and dedication and character.

The future is in our own hands!

An old wise man lived on the hilltop. Two little friends decided to fool him with a question that would flabbergast him. One of them held a tiny bird in his closed palm and asked the sage, 'Master, tell me whether the bird in my palm is alive or dead.' The master smiled and said, 'Son, if I say it is alive, you will smother it in your palm; if I say it is dead, you will open your palm and let it fly away. It is in your hands.' Yes, indeed, it is not the lines on our palm or our forehead but what we strive to achieve that matters. What matters most is to remember the fact: 'It is in our hands'. Our history is not our destiny.

EQUATION OF LIFE

In this temporal world, what matters is the simple equation: $B + \ldots + D = B$, where B is BIRTH, D is Death and what comes in between is most significant—C: CHOICE.

CHOICE and not CHANCE takes us to the goals set by us.

Destiny is not a matter of chance; it is a matter of choice. It is not a thing to be waited for, it is a thing to be achieved.

—WILLIAM JENNINGS BRYAN

When a couple is blessed with a baby, the parents put inserts for their friends in the newspaper, like: 'Mr and Mrs Blake have been blessed with a baby boy/baby girl.' In the journey of life, this baby traverses through years till he is put to rest in his grave. The person's gender is not written on the tombstone—no boy or girl. It says: 'Here lies…a doctor, a professor, a lawyer, a priest, a soldier, etc.' The choice was theirs. Almost 50 per cent of the millionaires in the world are not born with a golden spoon. They come from simple mediocre families and climb the ladder of success because they make the right choice.

How you get to the top matters most

Whenever one thinks of success, the image of a ladder against a wall comes to mind which one has to climb to the top. What is very important is not just the ladder but also the wall against which the ladder rests. Values matter, not just success.

THE RACE OF LIFE

In the race of life, it is not success of a job or business that empowers one; it is intrinsic. One has to walk the mile; there are no shortcuts. Life is a race; it is the desire to get to the goal. One has to remember that life is not about winning the race; life is about finishing the race. In this race, does competition matter? Yes, it does. Do not compete with anyone in the race of life. Compete with yourself. In the progress of life, one has to have self-confidence, courage and faith in one's abilities.

The average person goes to his worldly end with the music still in him. One of the human traits is to blame others or ourselves. 'I lost the match because I had a cramp in my hand'—this is the loser's limp. The loneliest race in life is that of a marathon; one has to run alone and compete with yours truly!

If one joins the rat race, one may end up being just a rat.

Roadblocks empower you

Beethoven achieved the impossible in music, although he was deaf. Stephen Hawking, who was literally immobile on his wheelchair, gave the world landmark features of science. Milton wrote the greatest epic—the masterpiece *Paradise Lost*, although he was almost blind. Impediments strengthen us—everything is in our hands, not on our palms. A blind man may have impaired vision, but in contrast, his auditory faculties are strong.

Obstacles are a part of life and that is what makes it interesting and a challenge. As a student in school, Richard was brilliant at everything, except history. He hated learning dates by rote and the names of the forefathers of the lineage of kings. He never knew his own lineage. His principal, who was a huge, burly man was feared by the children. They nicknamed him 'Bulldog'. Richard did well in all subjects, except history. His disinterest in this aspect of history made him loathe the subject. One day, Richard was summoned to the principal's residence next door while the principal was playing badminton with his dainty, petite wife. 'Come on, Richard, let's try to play badminton.' Richard sheepishly returned the shuttlecock, lest it hit Bulldog, which could land him in trouble. While playing, Bulldog asked him, 'Son, where did you learn to play badminton? Was there a stumbling block?' Richard promptly replied, 'Yes Sir, it was the net.' Bulldog turned around and asked him a pertinent question, 'Oh, so you learnt how to play badminton by removing the net?' Richard answered, 'No Sir, the game would not have been fun then.'

So, here was the lesson for Richard: History seemed to be a drab subject, telling us about dates, etc., but he got the message—if you want to have fun in life, appreciate the nets you face.

Four aspects lead to complete success

Right attitude + Skills + Character + Self-Image.
These four aspects must be underscored by perseverance.

The final analysis will depend not on a standard of life but by your standard of living. The world is made of two kinds of people—givers and takers. The takers may eat better, but the givers shall sleep better. How you treat others is how you are going to be treated by others.

Echo syndrome

Life is an echo. A little disgruntled boy who lived near a mountain was annoyed as his mother asked him to wait till she could afford to buy him a Rubik's cube. The boy went out to the mountain side and screamed: 'I hate you'. He ran back to his mother and said, 'Mama, there is a naughty boy living in the mountains who hates me; he screams at me, "I HATE YOU! I HATE YOU!"' The mother took her son to the mountain side and shouted: 'I LOVE YOU', and behold, the words echoed back: 'I LOVE YOU! I LOVE YOU!'

Life indeed is an ECHO… We get what we give.

In life, what you send out comes back; what you sow, you reap; what you give, you get; what you see in others, exists in you. Do not judge, lest you are judged. Give love and love comes back to you.

Failure is the condiment of success

A person disillusioned by life fails to overcome the battles. He must remember that one may lose a battle, but not necessarily the war. Sometimes we win, sometimes we learn. In fact, failure is the condiment of success. The best foundation of life is built on the stones hurled at us by others. The story of King Bruce is an exemplar. The king watched a spider trying to climb a wall but kept falling. It kept trying relentlessly and finally reached the top.

Most people think that the legend, Sir Hillary, scaled the Everest because it was there. Pinnacles are always there but the choice is to get there. Sir Edmund Hillary and Tenzing Norgay conquered Mount Everest in 1953. Not so, actually George Leigh Mallory, three decades earlier, was preparing to climb the Everest, but it was the duo—Sir Hillary and Norgay—that made it to the top. And after achieving the feat, out came the casual expression: 'We conquered the bastard.' We must set our goals, our own Everest; then we shall scale it for certain. Aim high and perhaps miss your target by a point rather than aim low and get there.

The NO factor

When one is looking for a job and comes back disappointed with the knife-like reply 'no', one fails to understand that the YES comes at the end of several NOs.

NO is not the end but a door opener to the Next Opportunity. The END is never there in all your attempts—the Effort Never Dies. The one who finally makes it realizes that several 'no', 'no', 'no' get us closer to a 'yes'. Just because one is a dropout from school does not mean that there isn't a world out there waiting for him. Steve Jobs became the czar of the Internet. What we need is just perseverance.

Decision-making

The most difficult word in the English language is NO. One finds it difficult to say 'no,' so he or she procrastinates in saying 'no' and gets the person at the other end nowhere. Decisions with revisions are no decisions.

Success seekers and failure avoiders

There are two categories—success-seekers and failure-avoiders. As Steve Jobs once said, 'You can't connect the dots looking forward; you can only connect them looking backwards.'

Believe

> *I think, therefore I am.*
>
> —RENÉ DESCARTES

In a school somewhere, there was a kid named Robin who was an over-sensitive child. Somehow, he did not apply his mind to the subjects he didn't like, such as history and mathematics. His math teacher was disappointed with his performance and would often say, 'Robin, you are a dud.' Robin believed him and dropped out of school.

He had to fend for himself without his formal education, so he took up menial jobs. Thirty years went by; Robin was stuck in the quagmire of his belief that he was a dud.

Suddenly, things changed. It happened on a Monday. An organization had sent the volunteers to take an Intelligence Quotient (IQ) test of the folks in and around the school. To the surprise of everyone, Robin had an the IQ of 160. Robin was congratulated and felicitated. Soon, he was asked to deliver lectures in different schools, institutions and corporate houses on how to rejuvenate people to get out from their state of hibernation. He was brilliant.

> *Criticism, like rain, should be gentle enough to*
> *nourish a man's growth without destroying his roots.*

> —FRANK A. CLARK

When Robin was told he was a dud, he believed it; when he was told he was a genius, he believed it.

> *NO ONE CAN HURT YOU UNLESS YOU*
> *GIVE PERMISSION TO BE HURT.*

To reprimand someone for a blunder, we should have three parameters:

1. Do it alone (or else we hurt his self-esteem)
2. Be firm
3. Let him leave with a feel-good factor (point out his strengths)

If you believe in yourself, the world above and below awaits you.

An elephant and a little sparrow were unusual friends. The elephant was always sad. One day, his little friend asked him, 'Why are you always sad?'

The elephant replied, 'Well, look, you can fly. You see the meadows, rivers, flowers and much more. Look at me—a hulk of flesh standing on the face of the Earth.'

The little bird replied, 'So you want to fly! Why didn't you tell me earlier?'

He then plucked a discarded feather from his tail, gave it to the elephant and said, 'Put it in your mouth, flap your ears hard and you will fly.'

The elephant did so and flapped his huge ears. Lo and

behold, he could fly!

When he returned, the elephant was ecstatic with joy and was ever grateful to the sparrow.

He said, 'Thank you, my little friend. It is because of you that I could fly!'

The sparrow smiled and replied, 'No, my dear friend, you did not fly because of me. You flew because you believed you could fly!'

YOU ARE WHAT YOU BELIEVE YOURSELF TO BE.

In your hands

The core of success is to remember that it is in your hands. You are the one that will be responsible to make or break it.

It is in your hands to create a better world for all who live in it.

—NELSON MANDELA

Richard Bach, in his modern allegorical masterpiece *Jonathan Livingston Seagull*, wrote about a lone seagull that believes in flying higher and higher. The eldest seagull admonishes him and reminds him that he has to fly only in quest of food. However, little Jonathan Livingston Seagull replies that he wants to reach heaven. The senior seagull laughs at him and retorts, 'There is no such place as heaven.' Jonathan replies, 'I know, heaven is not a Place. Heaven is not a Time. Heaven is being Perfect.'

You are what you believe yourself to be.

—PAULO COELHO

Believe and the burglar will come

A young couple who were madly in love finally tied the knot. They owned a duplex flat. The first evening, they had dinner downstairs, and as they were walking upstairs to retire for the day, the young wife turned around and told her Prince Charming, 'Darling, I think there is a burglar in the kitchen.' The man replied, 'We just came from the dining room and the kitchen.' But she sent him down to check, saying, 'When you were dating me, you said you will bring the stars and the moon down for me. In fact, you once said, "If I could catch a falling star, I would put it in a box, tie ribbons all around it and offer it to you."' The poor chap had to go down. He came back with the obvious answer, 'Darling, there is no burglar.'

But old habits die hard. So this became a routine practice every night as they walked up after dinner. Twenty-five years passed by and still the ritual and the belief of the wife that there was a burglar in the kitchen continued but to no avail. When it was their twenty-fifth wedding anniversary, the wife made the same request, 'Darling, there is a burglar in the kitchen!' The man reluctantly went down to the kitchen and behold, he actually saw a burglar!

He was happy and excited. He welcomed the burglar and said, 'My wife has been waiting for you for the past 25 years. Please wait; I will call her to meet you.'

IF YOU BELIEVE THE BURGLAR WILL COME,
HE WILL CERTAINLY COME.

*Faith is to beleive what you cannot see;
the reward of this faith is to see what you believe.*

—ST AUGUSTINE

Faith not only contradicts reason, it transcends it. If you believe, dreams become reality. But we must remember, dreams come true only when our eyes are open. Martin Luther King, in his immemorial speech 'I have a dream', did not just reiterate his faith in the future but also visualized it.

Don't let your dreams be dreams.

—JACK JOHNSON

In fact, your future is there for you to grab. It depends how you create it.

PEOPLE MANAGEMENT

A young mother was ready for a few minutes of relaxation after a long and demanding day. However, her young daughter had other plans for her mother's time.

'Read me a story, Mom,' the little girl requested.

'Give Mommy a few minutes to relax and unwind. Then I'll be happy to read you a story,' pleaded the mother.

The little girl was insistent that her mother read to her now. With a stroke of genius, the mother tore off the back page of a magazine which had the world map. As she tore it into several pieces, the mother asked her daughter to put the map together and then she would read her a story. Surely, this would buy her considerable relaxing moments.

A little while later, the girl announced the completion of her puzzle project. To her mother's astonishment, she found the world map completely assembled. When she asked her daughter how she managed to do it so quickly, the little girl explained that on the reverse side of the page was the picture of a girl. 'You see, Mommy, when I put the little girl together, the whole world came together!'

Life is a collage of many shades. The most difficult problem to solve are People Problems. Each of us has the responsibility to put our world together. It starts by putting ourselves together. We can become better parents, friends, spouses, employees and employers.

The first canon to handle people is to remain calm; don't get defensive. We need to control our environment. Most of all, one needs to remain focussed. Be as fair as possible. And of course, know when to back out. At the end of the day, we bet on people, not strategies.

THE 'WHAT IF' SYNDROME

One must not suffer from the 'what if' syndrome. It is significant to note that these lines from the poem entitled 'If' by Rudyard Kipling are written on the entrance at Wimbledon:

'If you can meet the triumphs and disaster

And treat those two imposters just the same;

….yours is the earth and everything that's in it…'

These lines sum up the ups and downs of life, the triumphs and disasters, which are but the shadow of a shade.

Anticipatory anxiety

Fear of the future is called Anticipatory Anxiety. 'What has been' and 'what might have been' points to one end and that is always the Present. Anticipatory Anxiety can also be a positive power to reckon with. It could trigger off the adrenalin.

Adversity is the grindstone of life. Intended to polish you up, adversity also has the ability to grind you down. The impact and ultimate result depends on what you do with the difficulties that come your way. Consider the phenomenal achievements of people experiencing adversity.

Sir Walter Raleigh wrote *The History of the World* during a 13-year-long imprisonment. If Christopher Columbus had turned back, no one could have blamed him, considering the constant adversity he endured on his voyages. Of course, no one would have remembered him either. Abraham Lincoln achieved greatness by his display of wisdom and character during the devastation of the Civil War. Martin Luther translated the Bible while enduring confinement in Wartburg Castle. Under a sentence of death and during 20 years in exile, Dante Alighieri wrote *The Divine Comedy*. John Bunyan wrote *The Pilgrim's Progress* in a Bedford jail.

Finally, consider a more recent example. Mary Groda-Lewis endured 16 years of illiteracy because of unrecognized dyslexia, was committed to a reformatory on two different occasions and almost died of a stroke while bearing a child. Committed to going to college, she worked at a variety of odd jobs to save money, graduated with her high school equivalency at 18, was named Oregon's Outstanding Upward Bound student and finally entered college. Determined to become a doctor, she faced 15 medical school rejections until Albany Medical College finally accepted her. In 1984, Dr Mary Groda-Lewis, at 35, graduated with honours to fulfil her dream.[2]

It's so hard to imagine that one of the most popular books—*Harry Potter* by J.K. Rowling—was rejected 12 times. It's such an inspiring example of why we should never give up.

Today, the inspiring man born without arms or legs, Nick Vujicic from Australia, has travelled to more than 57 countries, demonstrating how to reach beyond your goal. He gives us the elixir of being an OVERREACHER.

Every fall or setback strengthens us

Giraffes are tall. When a mother giraffe gives birth to a baby giraffe, the baby falls down from a height of seven feet. Mother giraffe stands over it and kicks it really hard.

The baby giraffe falls at a distance and tries to stand up again. Once again the mother giraffe comes and stands over it, licks it and gives it another hard kick.

The baby giraffe understands, 'If I don't act now, I will keep getting kicks.'

The baby giraffe starts trying to get up on its wobbly legs. Then, the mother kicks the baby again and the baby falls again. The baby understands, 'If I don't stand and run, I will be kicked again and again.' Now, the baby giraffe starts running; and at that moment, the mother comes and starts kissing and embracing the baby. The mother giraffe is aware that there are ferocious animals in the forest like tigers, wolves and many more who love to devour soft flesh of newborn animals. And the mother giraffe can't stay and protect the baby all the time.

---

[2]'Grind or Shine', *God's Work Ministry*, https://tinyurl.com/2yu2x4vw. Accessed on 30 April 2023.

Whenever challenges come your way, no matter how many times you fall, learn to get up. Learn from the baby giraffe to get up and stand, get up and start running.

Here's another example. A three-month-old infant was thrown into a swimming pool by a swimming trainer in Australia. The parents shrieked. But the baby beat its feet to stay above the water. The trainer explained the simple logic: The baby came from water, how can it drown in water!

Hopelessness is the biggest enemy of success.

We commit mistakes but every pencil has an eraser.

Move on. Erase the mistakes and make amends.

TRUST IS LIKE AN ERASER, IT GETS SMALLER AND SMALLER AFTER EVERY MISTAKE.

Do not look but see

Sometimes we look and do not see. Sometimes we see without looking. We often behold a blank slate and we fill it with what we think rather than what may be. In a flight to a foreign destination, a garrulous man made every effort to speak with his co-passenger to overcome the upcoming jet lag. The passenger had his nose literally dug into the inflight magazine. 'Hello' was not responded to. 'Where to, friend?' And the man did not respond. Awfully rude and discourteous he seemed to be. However, when the flight landed, the man tapped him on the shoulder to give him a piece of paper with a scribbled request: 'When we reach, kindly call this number…my wife's number… and tell her I will meet her in the lounge'. The co-passenger was deaf and dumb.

We look but do not see at most times.

Believe in the impossible

Every great achievement was once impossible until someone set a goal to make it a reality.

Lewis Carroll's famous masterpiece, *Through the Looking Glass*, contains a story that exemplifies the need to dream the impossible dream. In the book, there is a conversation between Alice and the Queen, which goes like this:

'I can't believe that!' said Alice.

'Can't you?' the Queen said in a pitying tone. 'Try again, draw a long breath and shut your eyes.'

Alice laughed. 'There's no use trying,' she said. 'One can't believe impossible things.'

'I dare say you haven't had much practice,' said the Queen. 'When I was your age, I always did it for half-an-hour a day. Why, sometimes I've believed as many as six impossible things before breakfast.'

When you dare to dream, many marvels can be accomplished. The trouble is that most people never start dreaming their impossible dream.

The songwriter Joe Darion wrote the song 'The Impossible Dream':

> 'To dream the impossible dream...
> this is my quest,
> to follow the star,
> no matter how hopeless,
> no matter how far.'

APPRECIATION MATTERS

It happened several years ago in the Paris Opera house. A famous singer had been contracted to sing there and ticket sales were booming. In fact, the night of the concert found the house packed and every ticket sold. The feeling of anticipation and excitement was in the air as the house manager took to the stage and said, 'Ladies and gentlemen, thank you for your enthusiastic support. I am afraid that due to illness, the man whom you've all come to hear will not be performing tonight. However, we have found a suitable substitute. We hope he will provide you with comparable entertainment.' The crowd groaned in disappointment and failed to hear the announcer mention the stand-in's name. The environment turned from excitement to frustration.

The stand-in performer gave the performance of his life. When he had finished, there was nothing but an uncomfortable silence. No one applauded. Suddenly, from the balcony, a little boy stood up and shouted, 'Daddy, I think you are wonderful!' Then the crowd broke into thunderous applause.

We all need people in our lives who are willing to stand up once in a while and say, 'I think you are wonderful.'

But one has to remember that it is a world of competition. James Baldwin, in his fourth novel titled *Tell Me How Long the Train's Being Gone*, wrote about a well-known artist on stage who suffered a stroke and had to be attended to in the wings of the stage. In the meantime, a substitute artist was called upon to keep the crowd engaged. By the time the well-known artist became ready to perform, the crowd refused to listen to him. They were interested in the substitute artist. Thus comes the title *Tell Me How Long the Train's Been Gone*.

Character matters most

The bottom line of success is character. Arthur Friedman wrote, 'Men of genius are admired, men of wealth are envied, men of power are feared, but only men of character are trusted.'

Fate is not what gets you there; you will get there if you master your faith.

I am the master of my fate; I am the captain of my soul.

—WILLIAM ERNEST HENLEY

If you believe, it will happen. Courage to continue counts.

*Success is not final. Failure is not fatal;
it is the courage to continue that counts.*

—WINSTON CHURCHILL

Success is an ongoing process. It is not about being the best, but about being better. And above and all, when you reach the pinnacle of success in whatever field you may be in, your signature becomes an autograph. Love what you are doing.

One has to love what one is doing in order to succeed. Success is not the key to happiness. Happiness is the key to success. If you love what you are doing, you will be successful.

—ALBERT SCHWEITZER

One of the priorities has to be education and continuous learning. Some of us speak years of experience in our core profession. Do years matter so much that they will convert a donkey into a horse? We have 25 years of experience, which may be just one year old. Upgrading your skills can help gain new opportunities and make you keep up with the times. TRY TO BETTER YOURSELF.

Don't try changing things; let's change us. This can transform losers into winners. This will prove to be like a 'miracle school'. This will be the gate to 'mission possible'. You will soon understand yesterday ended last night, today is your brand new day. The truth is loud and clear—success does not make you, failure doesn't break you. Faith, hope and love will replace anger, greed, guilt and envy. You will no longer look back in anger; you can look back in forgiveness and look forward to hope.

The road to one's destination does not stop abruptly. You didn't come this far only to come this far. You get what you focus on. Shirk negative thoughts. There are two crossroads where you can find two paths—the positive and negative. One path is to find an excuse and give up. The other one on your road to destination is to take up the mantle and find your way—act, don't procrastinate. Fear keeps us from achieving our dreams; it is action that conquers fear. Tomorrow is the feast of all fools. There are many times when we say 'let's do it tomorrow'. The biggest fault line is to believe that you have more time than you actually have—it is NOW or NEVER. Action counts. Don't wish for things to happen. Work for them.

EXCELLENCE BEYOND CLASS

Let us not chase perfection; let us strive for excellence. Ironically, failure is a big, if not the biggest, component of success. Believe it—we get what we want. Sounds easy, yet it requires us to believe and focus. We must all know our limitations and defy them. They are there for us to overcome all hurdles.

Re-look at the calender

One year does not simply mean 365 days; a year awaits us with 365 days of possibilities.

The best project awaits you

The best project to work on is at hand—grab it—it's YOU. Things don't just happen to you, they happen for you. Things may be rough at times, but believe in the fact that they cannot rough you up. Tough times don't last, tough people do. You can achieve anything, provided you give up the belief that you can't reach your goal.

Beware of peter principle

It is believed that people in a hierarchy tend to rise to a level of respective incompetence. Let's smile as we go up; if we come down in due course, others will also smile as we descend.

Humility is the key

Humility is all about having a positive attitude and being open to others. In a lighter vein—you scratch my back and I will scratch your back! Indeed, learn from others.

Humility is not thinking less of yourself,
it's thinking of yourself less.

—C.S. LEWIS

In fact, life is a long lesson in humility. The road to success is never easy. However, success is always sweet. If one wants to move on in the path to success, he must focus on goals, not on obstacles. Believing in yourself is the first secret to success.

It is usually the roughest road that leads to the heights of greatness.

—ZIAD K. ABDELNOUR

Sometimes in our quest on the road, we may get lost but that is not the end.

Some beautiful paths cannot be discovered without getting lost.

—EROL OZAN

The road to success is always under construction. Every individual aspires for growth all the time of his life; therefore, the road is always under construction. With time, there are changes—people change, situations change, and most importantly, human behaviour also changes. In order to commute on this road, which is always under construction, what is needed most are determination, hard work, reality, chance and values while walking on the path to success. In this long path to success, a person becomes compassionate, more responsible and more vigilant towards the goal. There are, in fact, three roads to success—yourself, your family and your profession. The first step in this road to success is setting the goal. Self-mastery and growth drives one to success. What is required is self-motivation to develop and grow. In fact, there are five stages of success:

1. Planning
2. Goal-setting
3. Research
4. Action
5. Scaling

The condiment to all this is one and only and that is hard work, and to be passionate and focussed on the goals set. One has to push the limits and be persistent. At the same time, one has to visualize the future. One has to keep in mind that the road to success is not straight. When obstacles arise, you may have to change direction. However, small steps can lead to a giant leap. One must stop being reactive; one must be proactive. Secondly, begin with the end in the mind. We must put the first things first, and above all, think win–win. We must synergize, and, most importantly, we must sharpen the axe before we use it.

There are several keys to success—commitment, an open mind, persistence, flexibility, faith, thankfulness, and, above all, passion. In order to travel the road to success, one needs to have a roadmap that includes a strategic plan and major steps or milestones needed to reach it.

All you need is a plan, the road map and the courage to press on to your destination.

—EARL NIGHTINGALE

Belief is what underscores success. Believe in yourself, in your job, show commitment, be an optimist, solve problems, follow your dreams, live with integrity, and, above all, show your passion and push yourself.

*ALL ROADS THAT LEAD TO SUCCESS HAVE
TO PASS THROUGH HARD WORK.*

Ironically, the road to success and the road to failure are almost exactly the same.

THE ROAD TO SUCCESS IS THROUGH COMMITMENT.

2

ATTITUDE

Attitude is a pattern of thinking. It is a mental as well as an emotional construct that affects behaviour and identity. Attitude is everything. A change in attitude ensures outcomes. A positive attitude is an asset.

A person with a positive attitude smiles when he wears out his shoes because he's back on his feet. When you fall, get up. One who complains that it is extremely hot or cold at work, ought to remember that we carry the weather within us when at work.

Attitude is contagious. We spread the virus of positive attitude wherever we go. Let's not join the band wagon of go-getters; let's join the club of go-givers.

One of the primary ways to strengthen your attitude is to make yourself a priority. What is required is positive affirmation—make your choices; be confident in your skills and gifts, and work towards your goals consistently.

Our attitude towards life determines life's attitude towards us.

—JOHN N. MITCHELL

APTITUDE VERSUS ATTITUDE

Attitude may be a little thing but it does make a difference.

It is not your aptitude but your attitude that will determine your altitude. A bad or negative attitude takes you nowhere.

A bad attitude can literally block love, blessing, and destiny from finding you. Don't be the reason you don't succeed.

—MANDY HALE

Attitude is just a way of thinking. So, change your thought process if you wish to change your attitude. 'The mind is in its own place, and in itself, can make a heaven of hell or a hell of heaven', wrote Milton. Yes, change your attitude and it will change your life. Your time is limited, so don't waste it by living someone else's life. When you have a dream, grab it; never let it go. Although life has got twists and turns, they should not become your impediments. You are never too old to set another goal or dream a new dream.

As time goes by, one must remember there is only one permanent thing in life—CHANGE.

Paradigm shift

We need to have a paradigm shift as we move along in changing times. We need to make a strategy. We need a fundamental change in approach underlying assumptions. It is an important change that happens when the usual way of thinking about or doing something is replaced by a new and different way. It is a major change in how one thinks and gets things done that replaces a prior paradigm. In the midst of a big move, a global pandemic and social unrest, there have been people who found a purpose. Paradigm shifts are found in the movement of scientific theory from the Ptolemaic system (the Earth at the centre of the universe) to the Copernican system (the sun at the centre of the universe) and the movement from Newtonian physics. Before, there had been the shift from paganism to monotheism.

We are living in a paradigm shift now, where information is getting increasingly freer. We want to restrict information on Facebook and other social media platforms with regard to offensive speech as the mainstream media won't be able to control it. But, people want to be allowed to have free opinion on gender, sexuality, religious groups and ethnicity.

One has to be open to change. This will work when we shift the angle of seeing. A paradigm shift occurs when new information significantly alters our thoughts and actions. In simple terms, a paradigm shift is a change from one way of thinking to another. What is around you can be looked at from either a positive or negative view. It is a kind of metamorphosis. It denotes a cognitive change. It denotes a dramatic new way of thinking or seeing something. The way we see the problem is the problem!

We are defined within the intersection of knowledge, skill and desire. Knowledge is the theoretical paradigm—*what to do* and *why*. Skill is about *how to do it*. Desire is motivation—*the want to do something*.

TEAM matters:

**TOGETHER
EVERYONE
ACHIEVES
MORE**

Initially, the paradigm is **YOU**—we say, 'Mom, you help me' or 'you do this for me', even if it means asking for shoelaces to be tied.

As we grow up, we become independent emotionally, mentally, physically and, of course, financially. The paradigm becomes **I**.

Finally as we progress to grow mature, we become interdependent. The paradigm becomes **WE**.

The very solar system is interdependent, and so are our personal and public life.

> *Out beyond ideas of wrongdoing and rightdoing,
> there is a field. I will meet you there.*
>
> —RUMI

There is a subtle difference between linear thinking and lateral thinking. Linear thinking is a safe process, whereas lateral (horizontal) thinking is risky, uneven and not widely accepted. While linear thinking is linked to the left side of our brain, lateral thinking is related to the right side of our brain. Both linear and lateral thinking are important. The theory about these two ways of thinking was propounded by Edward de Bono, a psychologist. It posits that linear thinking follows one path, uses existing knowledge methodically and is mostly applicable in solving mathematical problems; whereas, lateral thinking has different critical factors. We recognize the dominant ideas that polarize perceptions of a problem. It is a process by which we search for different ways of looking at things.

Let us demonstrate this anecdotally. A team of people decided to commute from one place to another. They sat for a brainstorming session to find ways to commute—storming the brain. The answers were multiple—walking, by metro, by railways, by helicopter, etc. The one who thought laterally suggested a tunnel be made that opens at the required destination. All other participants found it funny. Brainstorming should not be judgemental and, indeed, even today most bank robberies are done by tunnels that get into the banks. Similarly, perhaps some way a group of men sat down to decide how to make a vehicle that has different kind of wheels. The answers were all similar—it's got to be round. But the one who thought laterally believed it could be oval in shape. True enough, one of the most potent vehicles used in warfare is the tank, which has a kind of oval wheel setup.

STRATEGY TO FIGHT FAILURE

The fable about the race of a rabbit and a tortoise conveys the lesson that 'slow and steady wins the race'. The rabbit is overconfident in the race and rests midway beneath the shade of a tree and falls asleep. The tortoise overtakes him and slowly and steadily reaches the winning point. Then comes a strategy by the rabbit which is countered by a strategy of the tortoise who is now determined to win—which is required in all our planning.

The rabbit decides to have another race, and he makes sure he does not fall asleep and runs fast and steady. The tortoise agrees and the rabbit wins.

This time, with a strategy in mind, the tortoise invites the rabbit for another race. The rabbit agrees but the tortoise requests for a slight deviation on the path that leads to the victory point. This is the tortoise's new strategy. When they turn left at the crossroads, the rabbit is baffled; there is a pond which he has to cross. The tortoise, slow and steady, wins the race again.

Times have changed. When we heard of the term 'mickey' before, we always thought of Mickey Mouse. In today's cyber world, 'Mickey' denotes the speed of the mouse in your computer. Speed matters. Going back to the story and the strategy, the duo, i.e., the rabbit and the tortoise, plan to improve their timing by assisting each other. The rabbit makes the tortoise sit on his back and runs till the river. Thereafter, the rabbit sits on the back of the tortoise and crosses the river and they both make it to the winning point with a massive improvement in timing.

The essence of strategy is choosing what not to do

Strategy is the key to the art of performance. What not to do is more important than what to do.

A strategy is necessary because the future is unpredictable.

—ROBERT WATERMAN

> *If life were predictable, it would cease to*
> *be life, and be without flavour.*
>
> —ELEANOR ROOSEVELT

There are primarily three types of strategies—business strategy, operational strategy and transformational strategy. These three different strategies are crucial for success. The common factors in all three are people, processes and technology. Without them, strategy is just a set of lofty ideas. It helps us win and position ourselves against competitors.

Comfort zone

Comfort zone is a psychological state in which things feel familiar. It provides low levels of anxiety and stress. It is 'an anxiety neutral zone', says author Judith M. Bardwick.

Comfort zones describe a threshold of anxiety. It could be compared to wearing shoes that are not comfortable. We have to step out of our comfort zone if we ever want to grow.

> *A scholar who cherishes the love of comfort*
> *is not fit to be deemned a scholar.*
>
> —LAO TZU

A man sat by a river, waiting to catch a fish. Whenever he caught a large fish, he let it go, and when it was a smaller fish, he kept it for his meal. A passer-by noticed this act curiously. He could not resist knowing the answer. 'Why do you let the large catch go?' he asked. The man replied, 'What can I do? I have a small frying pan!'

Most people do not like to leave their comfort zone.

> *Many go fishing all their lives without
> knowing that it is not fish they are after.*

—HENRY DAVID THOREAU

Comfort zone is the enemy of prosperity. Get out of your comfort zone and face the challenges of life. The sky is the limit!

> *Life begins at the end of your comfort zone.*

—NEALE DONALD WALSCH

Once, in a certain garden, there were many little flowers among the big ones. In one corner, there was a very small flower, better say a neglected one. No one would notice it or care for it as everyone appreciated flowers like rose, lily, etc.

The small flower used to be very nervous. One day, he complained to God about his appearance and requested the Almighty to make him a rose. Other flowers told him not to change himself, but he didn't listen. At any cost, he wanted to be a rose because he saw the greatness of other roses very closely and he wanted to feel this greatness.

At last, the Almighty granted his request and transformed him into a rose. Now he became a rose and everyone appreciated him. At last, he was very happy with his new appearance. He was enjoying people's admiration. One day, there was a strong wind. Many flowering plants were uprooted. The small ones hid themselves in the bushes. The newly transformed rose was blown away by the wind. He was about to die. When he was taking his last breath, the other little flowers were laughing at him. They reminded him of their advice and made fun of him. The rose didn't mind it but he said, 'I am not sorry for losing my life, but I am proud that I am dying as a rose and not a neglected flower. I will die with peace of mind and satisfaction.'

Comfort zone is discomfort for us. A ship is comfortable at the shore, but it is made to challenge the waves, not to remain at the shore. So, hard work for success will make one achieve success. Stay in your zone too long and you lose the pleasure and gain the pain.

> *It's where you begin to think about going to your dream that your dream is always outside of your comfort zone. It's always beyond what you've ever done.*
>
> —BRUCE WILKINSON

Indeed, in the long run, our comfort zone becomes our uncomfortable zone. When you go out of your comfort zone and it works, there's nothing more satisfying. If your circle doesn't challenge you to grow beyond your zone, then you are definitely in the wrong circle.

Situations where one feels safe or at ease restrict us to a limited circle. It is a psychological state in which things feel familiar to a person and they are at ease and perceive they are in control of their situation.

To counter this weakness, one must train oneself with performance ability and a quest attitude.

Comfort zone may be classified into two types:

1. Habits of action
2. Habits of thinking

It could include your home, workplace, favourite restaurant or city of origin. Sometimes, those who travel a lot and open themselves up to new experiences are probably on their way to change their behavioural state.

We could classify three different zones in a person's life:

1. The comfort zone
2. The stretch zone
3. The panic (stress) zone

The first zone is a situation where one feels safe and at ease. This makes one avoid lots of anxiety as it is familiar ground. But it may prove to be a dangerous place. In order to get beyond this limited circle, one must be conscious of what is outside of this zone. Don't take yourself too seriously.

It is not easy to break out of your comfort zone. People around you will tear you down; however, remember the difference between a stadium full of cheering friends and an angry crowd screaming abuse at you.

I CAN'T, I CAN

In general, when it comes to attitude, people can be classified into two categories:

1. I CAN'T
2. I CAN

A person with a negative attitude remains in a problem; a person with a positive attitude concentrates on solutions—the first category focusses on what's missing; the second focusses on his or her blessings. One deals with limitations, the other with possibilities. You can't always control circumstances, but you can control your own thoughts.

Limitations live only in our minds. But if we use our imagination, our possibilities become limitless.

Taking a stand is the fortitude of a human being.

Whether you think you can, or think you can't—you are right!

—HENRY FORD

It is all in the mind—be it success or failure. We become what we think.

A man is what he thinks about all day long.

—RALPH WALDO EMERSON

SOMEBODY AND A NOBODY

Each one of us is a somebody; we were never born as a nobody. It is in our mind to build negativity and become a nobody!

A little boy in Texas was watching his father work as barber in his salon when a lone ranger rode up for a shave. As he looked in the mirror, he saw three gunmen with pistols; intentions that were not at all good or humorous. The agile lone ranger pulled out his pistol and pulled his trigger; and lo and behold, all the gunmen lay dead. After the ranger left, the little boy asked his Dad, 'Who was he?' The man replied, 'He is the best shot in Texas.' 'Is there any other shot like him?' The answer was crisp and terse, 'Nobody.' The boy took a comb and stood on the couch that lay on the side and yelled out, 'They call me NOBODY!' And soon he became the best shot in Texas. Yes, it's time we become a NOBODY!

Something is better than nothing. But the oxymoron is also not far away—nothing maybe everything.

A parent lovingly throws his little child up in the air and then holds him tight as he falls. What is significant is that the child smiles while falling because he believes that his father will hold him. Belief is the capstone of all motivation in life.

Many years ago, two salesmen were sent by a British shoe manufacturer to Africa to investigate and report back on market potential.

The first salesman reported back, 'There is no potential here. Nobody wears shoes.'

The second salesman reported back, 'There is massive potential here. Nobody wears shoes.'

This simple short story provides one of the best examples of how a single situation may be viewed in two quite different ways—negatively or positively.

We could explain this also in terms of seeing a situation's problems and disadvantages, instead of its opportunities and benefits.

When telling this story, its impact is increased by using exactly the same form of words ('nobody wears shoes') in each salesman's report. This emphasizes that two quite different interpretations can be made of a single situation.

You must first clearly see a thing in your mind before you can do it.

—ALEX MORRISON

If one can picture the way to success, it will come your way. I was born dumb, and for some strange reason, I was born in my father's library. After six years of silence, suddenly getting back the beauty of sound, I took to reading books for pleasure and became a talkative one for all. When people were thinking of the celluloid world, I discovered that a good book can be throttled in Hollywood. Good literature kindles the imagination; it does not satisfy it.

Imagination is more important than knowledge.

—ALBERT EINSTEIN

William Blake once wrote: 'I can see eternity in a grain of sand.' See and don't just look!

One has to have firm belief to smile in the journey of life; the elixir of life. Believe, if you wish to realize your dreams. The mundane draws us to Mother Earth; the clouds that hang from the sky beckon us to look above. The great Charlie Chaplin once aptly said, 'You will never find a rainbow if you are looking down.'

Don't create dark rooms within your mind, for in a dark room, even your shadow leaves you.

It is better to miss the impossible dream rather than not to dream. 'I have a dream'—spoken with conviction by Dr Martin Luther King Jr, has, in the course of time, become a reality. Now, it is not the colour of the skin but the content of character that matters. Today, the blacks and the whites sit at the common table of brotherhood. 'Yes, we can'—the signature tune of Barack Obama's election manifesto echoed across the democratic structure of America.

What is within is more important than what is without. Success is intrinsic.

It is all in the mind. Generally, we think of the price and the goal, but we forget the process. It is finally our mentality that gets us to our goal.

Don't compare yourselves to anyone in life. If you do so, you will be the saddest person in the world.

There is this story of an unhappy crow. The problem with him was that he was black. He was very sad because of his colour. So he was crying. Suddenly, a monk saw the crow crying and asked him the reason. The crow said, 'What to do if not to cry? No one likes me. No one likes a crow as a pet. No one gives me food. I spend most of my time in the garbage. God made me a crow and so I cry.'

The monk said, 'What do you want to become if you get another chance? I will make you that thing. I will fulfil your wish.'

The crow said, 'If I get another chance, I would like to be a swan, a white swan. What a beautiful colour—white, the symbol of peace.'

'Okay, I will turn you into a swan,' the monk said, 'But before that I want you to meet a swan at least once.'

The crow goes to meet the swan and says, 'Wow, brother, what a colour God gave you! You look amazing. You must be happy in life.'

The swan said, 'Who told you that I am happy?'

The crow asked, 'Are you not?'

'Not at all', the swan said.

'What's bothering you?' the crow asked.

'It's really the colour white. It's disgusting,' said the swan,

'No one likes white. White is basically the colour of the coffin.'

The two of them came back to the monk. The swan said, 'Give me one chance.'

The monk said, 'What do you want to become?'

The swan said, 'Make me a parrot. What a red lip, what a colour combination—green and red—the parrot has! People like to have parrots as pets. Parrots can also talk, so make me a parrot.'

The monk said, 'I will but before that go to the parrot and meet him once.' Now the trio went to the jungle and started searching for a parrot. They couldn't find one. After a lot of searching, they found a parrot and said to him, 'Wow, how amazing you are! What a colour, what a lip, just amazing! People pet you; they give you a name. How happy you are in life!'

The parrot said, 'Who said that I am happy?'

Swan asked, 'Are you not?'

'No', the parrot replied.

The swan asked, 'What's bothering you?'

The parrot said, 'My problem is my colour—green. Is it really a beautiful colour? It is the same as the jungle, the leaves and the trees. See, you were searching for me for a long time but could not find me because of my colour.'

Now the three of them returned to the monk. The monk asked, 'What do you want to become?'

The parrot said, 'A peacock. What an amazing bird! What a colour! When he dances, people take pictures of him.'

The monk said, 'I will turn you into one but before that go and meet the peacock once.'

Now all of them ran to meet the peacock and said, 'Wow, peacock, what an amazing life God gave you! When you open your feathers, people stare at you; they take pictures of you. People wait for you to open up your feathers because they like you; they want to see you dance. How happy you are, how amazing your life is!'

Finally, the peacock said, 'Who told you that I am happy? Listen carefully.' There was a sound.

The crow said, 'What's that sound?' It was the sound of a rifle being loaded.

The peacock said, 'It's the hunter. Every feather will be extracted one by one from my body and will be sold all over the world. People will buy and use my feathers to decorate their houses. Is it really a life? Why do you want to become me?'

'So you are not happy?' asked the crow.

'No', the peacock said.

The crow asked, 'Who's the happiest animal in the world?'

The peacock said, 'You!'

'How can I be happy?' said the crow. The peacock said, 'Have you ever heard of a crow burger or a crow sandwich?'

'No', said the crow.

'Did you see anyone sell crow's feather or meat?'

The crow said, 'No.'

'Do you live in any danger?'

The crow said, 'No.'

'Do you have trouble with anyone?'

'No.'

The peacock finally asked, 'So, tell me, who's living a great life, brother?'

Don't compare yourself with anyone. No one is better than you. God has not created another person like you. You are unique.

As a rule, man is a fool,
When it is hot,
He wants it cool.
When it is cool,
He wants it hot.
Always wanting,
What is not.

—BENJAMIN DISRAELI

Whenever business used to get slow, a balloon seller had a wonderful strategy to boost his sales. What the balloon seller used to do was release a helium-filled balloon into the air. When the children saw the colourful balloon go up, they all wanted one. They would come up to him with their parents, buy a balloon and his sales would go up. All day, he continued to release a balloon whenever sales were slow.

One day, when his balloon sales were low, he adopted the same strategy. He released a helium-filled blue coloured balloon into the air. As expected, the balloon man felt someone tugging at his jacket. He turned around and found a little boy smiling at him.

The balloon seller asked him, 'Which colour balloon do you want?' The innocent little boy looked at the helium-filled balloon into the air and asked with curiosity, 'If you release a black balloon, will it also fly?' Moved by the little boy's concern, the balloon man replied gently, 'My dear son, it is not the colour of the balloon; it is what's inside that makes it go up.'

We all want the home or hearth (destination) at the end of the day as the sun sets upon a distant hill. Is home a place or is it much more?

An artist wanted to paint the most beautiful picture in the world. He wondered what the most beautiful thing in the world was. In his inquisitiveness, he asked a newly married bride and she replied promptly: 'LOVE'; a weary soldier said the most beautiful thing is 'PEACE' and a practising priest replied: 'FAITH'. The artist wondered where he would find these three elements of beauty—love, faith and peace. As he walked into his home, he saw LOVE in the eyes of his wife; FAITH in the eyes of his children and PEACE was the place that he found there amidst love and faith. He then painted the most beautiful thing in the world and below the painting he wrote: MY HOME.

As one traverses the ups and downs of life, not only does one want the cash bells ringing in his bank account but he also wants a strong bank balance in his relationship with all. Bankruptcy in motivation will not take one to the milestone set in one's life. You need the fuel and the fire to get you there.

What matters is your mental attitude—your mental reaction to people, circumstances, conditions and objects. Your emotional quotient must gel with your cold and calculative plans. The solar plexus and the cerebral cortex need equilibrium.

There are people who look and cannot see; there are people who can see without looking. Insight is what heads one's attitude.

Vision is the art of seeing what is invisible to others.

—JONATHAN SWIFT

We all have within us a coat of many colours, i.e., dreams. It is a fact that dreams come true with your eyes open.

> *If you can dream it, you can do it.*
>
> —WALT DISNEY

If you believe, you can move mountains. Efforts will fully give us rewards if a person decides and refuses to quit.

> *With ordinary talent and extraordinary perseverance,*
> *all things are attainable.*
>
> —THOMAS BUXTON

TOO MUCH, TOO LITTLE

Being happy, even when you have little, will take you to a positive station between 'too much' and 'too little'.

Once upon a time, a fisherman was sitting near a river, beneath the shadow of a tree and lazily smoking a pipe. A rich man, who was passing by, stopped and inquired why he was sitting under a tree and smoking and not working. To this, the fisherman replied that he had caught enough fish for the day. The rich man retorted with a question, 'Why don't you catch more fish instead of sitting in a shadow wasting your time?'

The fisherman replied with a question, 'What would I do by catching more fish?'

The businessman replied, 'You could catch more fish, sell them, earn more money and buy a bigger boat.'

The fisherman replied with a question, 'What would I do then?'

'You could go fishing in deep waters, catch even more fish and earn even more money,' replied the businessman.

Pat came the question from the fisherman, 'What would I do then?'

The businessman, with his financial acumen, replied, 'You could buy many boats, employ many people under you and earn even more money.'

The fisherman replied with his staple question, 'What would I do then?'

'You could become a rich businessman like me.' Pat came the question, 'What would I do then?' The businessman replied, 'You could then enjoy your life peacefully.'

The fisherman smiled and replied, 'What do you think I am doing right now?'

LIFE IS A FULL CIRCLE; IN MY BEGINNING IS MY END AND IN MY END IS MY BEGINNING.

Having a good time, even when you are losing, will uplift your spirit. Being happy for someone else's success will also add an aspect of positivity in you.

Power of appreciation

1. Listen to your internal dialogue. When faced with a negative thought, turn it around to make it into a positive thought.
2. Interact with positive environments and with positive people.
3. Volunteer.
4. Get pleasure out of the simple things in life.
5. Permit yourselves to be loved.
6. Change your perspective.
7. Smile and be kind to others.

8. Practise self-compassion.
9. Don't take things personally.
10. Be happy for other people's success.

CONTROL YOUR ATTITUDE

1. Avoid negative news.
2. Realize that your attitude is entirely up to you.
3. Be grateful for everything good in your life.
4. Keep the big picture in mind.

Positive attitude is the key to success

A positive attitude helps you cope more easily with the daily affairs of life. It brings optimism in your life and makes it easier to avoid worries and negative thinking. If you adopt it as a way of life, it would bring constructive changes in your life and make it happier, brighter and more successful.

What makes a good attitude—being optimistic about situations, interactions and ourselves.

You learn to deal with disappointments and failures more easily. You will be more empathetic and understanding towards others. You will be more grateful.

The three Ps are the stepping stones to success.

> *Patience, persitence and perspiration make an unbeatable combination for success.*
>
> —NAPOLEON HILL

What we sometimes miss can prove to be futile

Once there was an aged tea-maker who worked at the railway station. He and his wife were always sad because they were not blessed with a child. They wanted to have a son who could look after them in their old age.

While he was waiting, he noticed that an old couple had been sitting on the platform since morning. In his curiosity, he went and inquired, 'Is there a train that you have been waiting for since morning?'

'No,' the old man sitting on the bench looked up and replied, 'Actually, we are waiting for my elder son. When we boarded the train, my younger son told us that his elder brother will come and pick us up.'

'Do you know your elder son's address?' the tea-maker inquired.

'We are illiterate. We cannot read. Here is his address.' The old man handed him a paper with something written on it. The note had a surprising message: 'Whosoever reads this message, please take my parents to the nearest old age home.'

The irony of having children or not having children can be startling. So is the story of a man who was about to breathe his last in a hospital. His two sons were planning for his funeral. The first suggested that they should hire an ambulance or a hearse to the burial ground.

'That would cost us a lot of money,' said the other son.

Then came the next suggestion, 'After he's no more, let's put him on the bike. I will ride and you hold him.'

'What about the cost of the fuel? And then we have to get the bike serviced and washed. That would also cost money.'

Hearing all this, the old man stood up and said, 'Throw

me my slippers. I'll go on my own!'

The message is loud and clear for all: I WILL GO ON MY OWN.

Would you like to exchange your struggles with others?

Problem-solving is always better than exchanging problems with others.

The road to a happier and more successful life starts with your attitude—when your attitude is within your control.

One has to nurture three powerful steps:

1. Think
2. Speak
3. Act

Think—success begins in the mind.
Speak—watch your words.
Act—don't sit back.

I am not saying a positive attitude will make you successful,
I am saying a positive attitude can make you successful.

—NORMAN VINCENT PEALE

Attitude reflects in what you say and do. A negative attitude can make you say things like 'it doesn't really matter' (carelessness), 'if it happens, it happens' (fatalism), 'I didn't fall sick for so many years, I won't fall sick now' (overconfidence), 'It's so much trouble to wear sunglasses and a hat together' (laziness), 'I didn't know this would happen' (ignorance), 'all these self-help books are kids' stuff' (cynicism), etc.

Stop complaining and move ahead.

Troubles, like babies, grow larger by nursing.

—LADY HOLLAND

BEYOND BOUNDARIES

Boundaries suggest rules and restrictions. Parents, teachers, peers and supervisors formulate these boundaries. And they holds us accountable, so that we remain within boundaries. That isn't a bad thing. Beyond the boundaries is something different. Think of those leaders, teachers, supervisors and parents who inspire us to go beyond the call of duty, to do more than what we have to do—not because they tell us to but because we want to.

BE EMPOWERED

How can we inspire people and ourselves to be self-motivated? The key word is EMPOWERMENT. In management terms, it is a simple direction: Get it done. With fewer resources and time, get it done. Feeling empowered is different. It is the time when you are self-motivated.

Try to answer these three questions:

1. Can you do it? Do you believe you can do it? Do you have the knowledge and training to do it?
2. Will it work? It is a kind of response efficacy. In elementary school, we call it education; in higher school–education, in university–higher education. When you go to an industry, it is called training. Training means you do the required behaviour and get feedback. Online training appears to be an oxymoron;

it is not hands-on training.
3. Is it worth it? If we answer all three questions with a 'yes', we will become competent. Competence comes from feedback and recognition.

> *The gretest glory in living lies not in never falling,*
> *but in rising everytime we fall.*
>
> —NELSON MANDELA

There are two kinds of people:

1. Success-seekers
2. Failure-avoiders

A failure-avoider goes to attend the class, so that he does not fail. The paradigm is negative. A success-seeker goes beyond the frontiers of limitations and excels.

Help yourself

Ralph Waldo Emerson said, 'Do the thing you fear and the death of fear is certain.' In case one runs away from one's fear, it is a losing strategy. Confront your fears and you shall move ahead.

> *The only thing we have to fear is fear itself.*
>
> —FRANKLIN D. ROOSEVELT

> *Two things define you: your patience when you have nothing*
> *and your attitude when you have everything.*
>
> —GEORGE BERNARD SHAW

Life is full of ups and downs. Sometimes, circumstances are out of control. It is hard to fight the 'glass is half-empty' mentality when life feels more dark than light. One way to bring more positivity in life is by connecting with people.

If you look the right way, you can see that the whole world is a garden.

—FRANCES HODGSON BURNETT

Building a positive attitude begins with having confidence in yourself.

The most important thing you will ever wear is your attitude.

—JEFF MOORE

Happiness is next door. Adjust your attitude if you want life to be happier. If you hold a glass, it may not be heavy. If you hold the glass all day long, it may cramp your hand. Similarly, our worries and stressful thoughts, if held for long, will cramp us too.

Most people make themselves unhappy simply by accepting how they feel. Don't allow feelings to reduce you. Use you struggles and frustrations to motivate yourself. Even when you are upset, don't be hateful. Happiness and a negative mindset cannot co-exist. We stand between two options—either we make ourselves miserable or we make ourselves strong.

On the road to success, we learn the way on the way. Think of all the steps and missteps and chances and coincidences that have got you there.

Learn to forgive

Unless we learn to forgive ourselves, unless we forgive the situation, unless we accept the situation that is over, we cannot move ahead. We must learn to let go. Comprehend the past with wisdom and strength.

Stepping on to a new path is difficult, but not more difficult than remaining in a situation. Keep your heart open to better times on the road ahead.

Quality assurance matters. One of the leading associates of quality was Philip Crosby. He proclaimed, 'Quality is free. It is cheaper than fixing it later. It has nothing to do with good or bad. What matters is performance to requirement.'

Work towards zero defect

After all, we are human. How can we have zero defects?

'To err is human' is a way to justify defects—'I was late, as there was a traffic jam'; 'I was late because I had a late night'…so on and so forth. But when you have to board a flight, there can be no display of defect! And you dare not keep your bride-to-be waiting, or she will walk down the aisle with someone else!

In our approach to attitude, time matters a lot. In fact, time is a limited resource. Once it is gone, it is gone. Time management helps you prioritize your tasks. Your quality of work improves and it lowers your stress. Create a to-do list and meet it regularly. Try to minimize distractions. Procrastination can be a virus. Battle procrastination. At the end of the day, do review your task list.

Change the way you look at yourself

There are five ways to work on this aspect:

1. List your personal liabilities, past mistakes, failures, embarrassments and burn the list.
2. List your personal assets and value them.
3. Read inspiring and motivational stories to rejuvenate yourself.
4. Write specific goals and keep looking at them.
5. Be responsible for the nuances of your emotions.

Dos and don'ts when looking above your need

- Go above and beyond expectations.
- Bring solutions, not more problems.
- Bounce back from mistakes.
- Don't make excuses.
- Don't depend on reminders to complete your work.
- Work for improvement, not perfection.
- Think ahead.
- Don't dwell on successes.
- Don't assume too much.
- Negotiate agreements and then get going.

Maximizing performance

FOR SUCCESS, ATTITUDE IS EQUALLY IMPORTANT AS ABILITY.

One must develop character, foresight, self-reliance and courage. Assuming responsibility may be hard, but it pays in the long run.

Pre-empt your decision

- Take time to think things through.
- For each possible solution, list the possible good and bad.
- Be objective and look at the facts.
- Keep your preconceptions, prejudices and personal dislikes out of your decision-making.
- Face the fact that criticism is inevitable.

If you fail to prepare, you prepare to fail

In simple terms, there are three aspects that make up a complete man. When Siddhartha, in the novel by the same name written by Herman Hesse, was asked by a businessman what he could do, he gave a terse reply: 'I can read. I can write. I can think.' We need to think, re-think and re-structure our attitude as we progress towards success.

Progress almost always requires change. Your attitude will prepare you for this and help you adjust to change. We need to overcome resistance to change.

3

THE POWER OF SKILLS

Excellence is not a skill, it's an attitude. But do note—when love and skill work together, expect a masterpiece. Every skill you acquire doubles your chances of success. There are two dimensions to skills—soft skills and hard skills. Hard skills refer to your technical ability and knowledge of facts; soft skills allow you to more effectively use your technical knowhow. Soft skills can also be thought of as 'people skills'. These can include good communication and interpersonal skills, leadership, problem-solving, work ethic, time management and teamwork. These are characteristics that can be carried over to any position.

There are several hard skills, too. One is, of course, computer skills, especially proficiencies in operating specific software or applications. The other hard skills could be categorized as technical skills, marketing skills, writing skills, design skills, analytical skills and language skills.

The hard skills, one has to hone himself or herself. However, there can be nothing with finite perfection. People think computers will keep them from making mistakes. They're wrong. Ironically, with computers, you make mistakes faster. With no affront suggested, GOOGLE is the result of the misspelling of GOOGOL—1 followed by 100 zeroes. However, while we cannot deny the fact that computers were born to solve problems, their limitation in certain facets also cannot be denied.

A COMPUTER ONCE BEAT ME AT CHESS, BUT IT WAS NO MATCH FOR ME AT KICK-BOXING

Soft skills are personality traits such as leadership, communication and time management. One of the primary aspects of soft skills is creativity. Creativity has nothing to do with fine arts. One can be creative even while cleaning a house. Creativity is finding alternatives in a given situation. This, in turn, puts us into a positive framework of adaptability. It helps us in problem-solving.

A child who visits a zoo and has to write a paragraph on his experience will traditionally have a template that will answer these questions: when, where, why, how and what. The information shall be informative but drab. A creative child writes a paragraph in a different way. He writes of a lone lion in a cage, who is almost asleep, with flies buzzing around his nose. A naughty little boy throws a stone at him. The lion growls and looks up at the sky. The creative child will interpret this as the lion saying to the heavens: 'My Father, forgive these children for they know not what they do.'

The three basic categories of skills in the world are—knowledge, transferrable skills and self-management skills.

Verbal communication and written communication form the core, along with emotional intelligence.

When we speak, we may hurt people unknowingly. The defense is a one-liner—it was a 'slip of the tongue'. The logic is quite weird. The tongue is in a wet place, so it slips regularly. A wrong word could sabotage beautiful relationships.

Every word, be it in any language, is sacrosanct. The gospel of St John opens with these significant lines: 'In the beginning was the Word, and the Word was with God, and the Word was God.' The secret of effective speaking is almost an oxymoron—talk less, speak more. There are three S's of public speaking—stand up, speak up, and, the most important, shut up. Many speakers do not know when to end talking, and, ultimately, their verbosity becomes jarring. Sometimes, writers and speakers suffer from an unusual symptom of logorrhea—a diarrhoea of words. Ironically, the most powerful way of expressing your thoughts and speaking could be silence.

Today, we embrace digital transformation with zeal. Efficiency works only when you can predict what you may need. When the unusual comes along, efficiency is no longer your friend. The crucial aspect is how to deal with the unexpected. The unexpected is becoming the norm. In the past 20 to 30 years, the world has moved from being complicated to complex. Yes, there are patterns but they do not repeat themselves. Expertise will not suffice because the system keeps changing too fast. So, there are now a huge number of changes that defy forecasting. Efficiency is no longer our guiding principle. In the past we had 'just in case' management; this has been replaced by 'what if it happens'. We know the pandemic will come again, but we cannot avert it. But, certainly, we can prepare for this calamity. We must all have poise and skills for these unexpected uncertainties.

Preparedness, imagination building and experiments ought to be the need for the new approach to an unknown zone of skills.

In an unpredictable age, we need resilience and strength. They aren't efficient but they give immense capacity for preparedness, experiment and bravery. They give us adaptation.

The human skills we need in an unpredictable world is the crux. To predict the future requirement of skills is hallucination. We ought to know that preparedness is at the core of all skills today. We are brave enough to invent things that are yet to come. Hone and develop your skills and then you can make anything of the future.

Mark Twain says there are two significant days in our lives—the first is the day that we were born, and the second is the day we understand why.

There is a gap between the people who are training folks and those who will employ them.

Today, digital literacy happens to be the most needed skill of the times. Online education, along with face-to-face education, is the need of the day. We are now in the midst of change.

The three human skills needed for the future are loud and clear. First, **creativity**—it is about looking at the world differently, trying new things and experimenting with new ideas. Creativity is a very human skill. It cannot be the output of machines. Second is **communication**. Public speaking initially can be an uncomfortable experience. Public speaking is not a world of spiders and snakes. But it is like a phobia most people suffer from. Straight and simple—when we speak to someone there are no inhibitions; the moment the numbers increase, it becomes public speaking. Public speaking is absolutely the need of the present and the future. You cannot learn this from textbooks. Only by speaking do you learn to speak. The third important skill is **financial literacy**. Understanding the fundamentals of tax is a must for every human being. Beware of the greatest temptation—buy now and pay later; there are hazards and financial risk factors of credit cards. Earlier, on a date, we used to give our fiancé a red rose—a symbol of love. Today, most probably, she will expect something different—an add-on credit card!

We need fresh new thinking when it comes to skills.

Excellence is not a skill, it's an attitude.

—TONY ROBBINS

COMMUNICATION

Communication is as much of an attitude as it is a technique. Four essential communication skills are as follows:

- Written communication—to convey ideas and communication through the use of written language
- Oral communication—to convey ideas and information to the user through spoken language
- Non-verbal and visual communication
- Active listening and textual communication

Communication must have a purpose and should be constructive. Focus on the topic you are speaking on, share information and, above all, follow the maxim—when in doubt, cut it out!

Communication is the process of sharing information, knowledge or meaning. What matters most is 'response-ability'. Response is more important than the message.

Two little boys wanted to find out the secret of wisdom. So, they decided to go up the mountain where a wise hermit lived. One of them asked the hermit, 'Sir, what is the key to wisdom?'

The wise man replied, 'Listen, my son.' He then fell silent. The two boys waited eagerly to collect the gems of wisdom.

After a long pause, one of boys asked the teacher, 'Master, we are listening; please continue.'

The sage smiled and said, 'There is nothing else to be said.' Indeed, one needs a lot of courage to speak, but one needs even greater courage to sit down and listen. There are two kinds of listeners. The first category is generally more in number—they listen to get an answer. The second category simply listens. When we listen, there is a message that we convey to the speaker—I care.

Zeno of Citium once said, 'We have two ears and one mouth, so we should listen more than we say.'

We speak an average of 150 words per minute. But our mind, with its billions of cells, can process almost a 1,000 words per minute. Yes, there is much more to listening than meet the ears.

Listening is an art that requires attention over talent, spirit over ego, others over self.

—DEAN JACKSON

One of the most sincere forms of respect is actually listening what another person has to say.

So you think listening is easy!

To begin to be a good listener, most people think communication is speaking or writing. Indeed, they are essentials. Being a better listener is what matters. Active listening is essential. Do not listen to reply; listen to listen actively. The skills of listening are essential. Within the portals of our schooling and higher education, it is taken for granted that listening comes naturally. No, not true. One has to train oneself in the skill of listening.

Only when we listen do we get clarity. It helps to understand meaning and interpretation; it helps in understanding matters and above all we get feedback, too.

Listening requires much effort, it needs hard work. Mostly we hear, but we do not listen. Our mind wanders over several issues and we really fail to listen. The human mind can process many times faster than anyone can talk. We generally 'hear' what our mind dictates, not what is being told to us.

Mostly, the last few words spoken are picked up by our faculty of listening. We may look at the forest and miss the tree!

The elements that make you a good listener are several. Look at the speaker—eye contact is essential in signaling that you are listening. Your facial expression will be the sign that you are listening. Don't interrupt is the first commandment for being a good listener; and, above all, be an emphatic listener. The power of a good question endorses the fact that you have been listening. Asking is not telling—sometimes, we may need more information.

Remember: The tongue has no bones, but it is strong enough to break a heart. So, we must be careful with our words.

> *We need to think of our tongue as our messenger*
> *that runs errands for our heart.*
> *Our words reveal our character.*

—CHUCK SWINDOLL

We must try not to mix bad words with our bad mood. You will certainly have many opportunities to change the mood, but you will never get the opportunity to replace the words that you spoke. It is very important to talk with our mind before we talk with our tongue. As the teaching goes—want to be respected? Just control your tongue. We have to be mindful of our words. They can either heal or hurt, with lasting effects.

> *Fill your mind before you empty your mouth.*

—HABEEB AKANDE

It was the Noble Laureate Rabindranath Tagore who once wrote: 'Gray hairs are signs of wisdom if you hold your tongue, speak and they are but hairs, as in the young.'

William Shakespeare also aptly wrote: 'Give every man an ear, but few thy voice.'

The world of correspondence today is very different from the olden days when the postman rang the bell and all at home ran to receive the little letters that came for them. Today, the envelope and the postage stamp are on their way out. The major mode of communication is email. The epitome of a good email is KISS—Keep it Short and Simple. In life, what gives a person finesse is etiquette. In the cyber world, it is netiquette.

Netiquette tips

- Make sure your email includes a courteous greeting and closing line. This helps to make your email not seem demanding or terse.
- Address your contact with the appropriate level of formality and make sure you spell their name correctly.
- Do a spellcheck. Emails with typos are not taken seriously.
- Read your email out loud to ensure that the tone is one that you desire. Try to avoid relying on formatting for emphasis; choose words that reflect your meaning. Addition of words such as 'please' and 'thank you' goes a long way.
- Be sure you include all relevant details or information necessary to understand your request or point of view. Generalities may cause confusion.
- Are you using proper sentence structure? Are you capitalizing the first word and using appropriate punctuation? Multiple instances of '!!!' or '???' are perceived as rude or condescending.
- If an email is emotionally charged, walk away from the computer and review it before replying. Review the sender's email again and make sure that you are not reading into anything that simply isn't there.
- If sending attachments, did you first ask the receiver when would be the best time to send them? Did you check the file size to make sure you don't fill the receiver's inbox, causing subsequent email to bounce?
- Refrain from using the 'Reply to all' feature to give your opinion to those who may not be interested. In most cases, replying to the sender alone is your best course of action.
- Make one last check that the address or addresses in the 'To' field are those you wish to reply to.

- Be sure that your name is reflected properly.
- Type complete sentences. Random phrases or cryptic thoughts do not lend to clear communication.
- Never assume the intent of an email. If you are not sure, always ask to avoid unnecessary misunderstandings.
- Just because someone doesn't ask for a response, doesn't mean you ignore them. Always acknowledge emails from those you know in a timely manner.
- Be sure that the 'Subject' field accurately reflects the content of your email.
- Don't hesitate to say, 'Thank you', 'How are you?' or 'Appreciate your help'.
- Keep emails brief and to the point. Save long conversations for the telephone.
- Always end your emails with 'Thank you', 'Sincerely' and 'Best regards'.

Communication is power. Human behaviour and feelings find their original roots in some aspects of communication. It does not just mean speaking but also includes listening.

> *The most important thing in communication is to hear what hasn't been said.*
>
> —PETER DRUCKER

By failing in comprehending communication, we fail to understand the other person's feelings. Listening can be hazardous when our approach is wrong. The biggest communication problem is that we do not listen to understand; we listen to reply.

There is a subtle distinction between 'what you say' and

'how you say it'. 'A good morning' necessarily doesn't mean good, if you wish somebody with a foul tone. Your intonation says a lot. A 'thank you' could just be a formal expression or it could be a real expression of gratitude.

The beauty of life is in the hurdles. Several problems crop up in an organization such as planning, finance and performance. Every problem has a solution, but the most difficult problem is the PEOPLE PROBLEM.

The blind man and the advertising story

An old blind man was sitting on a busy street corner during rush-hour, begging for money. On a cardboard sign, next to an empty tin cup, he had written: Blind—Please help.

No one gave him any money.

A young advertising writer walked by and saw the blind man with his sign and empty cup, and also saw the many people passing by completely unmoved.

The advertising writer took a thick marker pen from her pocket, turned the cardboard sheet back-to-front, rewrote the sign and then went on her way.

Immediately, people began putting money into the tin cup.

After a while, when the cup was overflowing, the blind man asked a stranger to tell what the sign now said.

'It says,' said the stranger, 'It's a beautiful day. You can see it. I cannot.'

With these words, the magic worked.

Use simple language. Do not use five words when one would do. Use positive words. Avoid words like 'but', 'try', 'maybe', etc.

Words are the clothes that thoughts wear.

—SAMUEL BECKETT

Tips for correct speaking

When you speak, remember there are two aspects:

- What you say
- How you say it

'I need your help', says your boss, walking up to your desk. Is it an ORDER, a COMMAND, a REQUEST or a COMPLIMENT?

Conversation is partly self-expression. It provides us opportunities for asserting our individuality, telling the world how we feel.

At its best, conversation means pooling information, sharing interests and bringing together ideas.

Speech is power: speech is to persuade, to convert, to compel.

—RALPH WALDO EMERSON

It was once said a good speech is like a pencil; it has to have a point.

Seven ways to be a good conversationalist

- Be interesting
- Be friendly
- Be cheerful
- Be animated yet relaxed
- Be flexible

- Be tactful
- Be courteous

Eight don'ts of a conversation

Don't be:

- Dogmatic
- Condescending
- Argumentative
- Lifeless
- Insincere
- Egocentric

The six most important words:
I ADMIT THAT I WAS WRONG.
The five most important words:
YOU DID A GREAT JOB!
The four most important words:
WHAT DO YOU THINK?
The three most important words:
COULD YOU PLEASE?
The two most important words:
THANK YOU
The one most important word:
WE
The least important word:
I

Miscommunication

A man and his wife had been arguing all night; and as bedtime approached, neither was speaking to the other. It was not unusual for the pair to continue this war of silence for two or three days; however, on this occasion, the man was concerned. He needed to be awake at 4.30 a.m. to catch an important flight, and being a very heavy sleeper, he normally relied on his wife to wake him up. Cleverly, or so he thought, while his wife was in the bathroom, he wrote on a piece of paper: 'Please wake me at 4.30 a.m. I have an important flight to catch.' He put the note on his wife's pillow, then turned over and went to sleep.

The man awoke the next morning and looked at the clock. It was 8.00 a.m. Enraged that he'd missed his flight, he was about to go in search of his errant wife to give her a piece of his mind, when he spotted a hand-written note on his bedside cabinet. The note read: 'It's 4.30 a.m. Get up.'

When you speak, you must speak from your heart. Authenticity and sincerity are what matter. When one does not speak with genuine thought, it may sound hollow.

You can speak well if your tongue can deliver the message of your heart.

—JOHN FORD

Saying thanks

Charles Plumb was a navy jet pilot. On his seventy-sixth combat mission, he was shot down and parachuted into enemy territory. He was captured and spent six years in prison. He survived and now on the lessons he learnt from his experiences.

One day, a man approached Plumb and his wife in a restaurant, and asked, 'Are you Plumb, the navy pilot?'

'Yes. How did you know?' asked Plumb.

'I packed your parachute,' the man replied.

Plumb was amazed and grateful, 'If the parachute you packed hadn't worked, I wouldn't be here today...'

Plumb refers to this in his lectures—his realization that the anonymous sailors who packed the parachutes held the pilots' lives in their hands; and yet the pilots never gave these sailors a second thought; the pilots never even said hello, let alone offer thanks to these sailors.

Now, Plumb asks his audiences, 'Who packs your parachutes? Who helps you through your life...physically, mentally, emotionally and spiritually? Think about who helps you; recognize them and say thanks.'

THERE ARE MANY WE MEET WHO ARE JUST PASSING THROUGH, AND THEN THERE ARE A FEW, WHO STAY TO PULL US THROUGH.

TEAMWORK

There was once a man who lived with his three sons. His sons were hard workers, but they constantly fought with each other.

Even though the man continuously tried to help his sons make peace with each other, he was never successful. In fact, their fighting got to a point where their neighbours would make fun of them.

Eventually, the father became ill. He begged his sons to learn how to work together because of his impending death, but they didn't listen. The father then decided to teach his sons a practical lesson to help them forget their differences and become a united team.

The father called his sons and said, 'I'll give you each an

equal number of sticks to break in half. Whoever breaks the sticks the fastest, will be rewarded.'

After the sons agreed to do the task, the father gave each of them 10 sticks and instructed them to break each stick in half.

This task took the sons mere minutes to complete, but once they were finished, they started to fight about who finished first.

The father said, 'Dear sons, the task isn't finished. Now I'll give each of you 10 more sticks, however, you must break the sticks in half as a bundle rather than snapping each one separately.'

His sons agreed and attempted to do what he asked. Each son tried his best, but none could break the bundle in half.

They told their father that they had failed.

In response, their father said, 'See, it was easy to break the sticks in half individually, but you couldn't break all 10 of them at the same time. Similarly, if the three of you stay united as a team, nobody will be able to harm you. However, if you fight all the time, anyone will be able to defeat you. Please come together as a united team.'

Alone, we can do so little; together, we can do so much.

—HELEN KELLER

We are not a team because we work together. We are a team because we respect, trust and care for each other.

Anger management

There was once a boy who became angry so frequently with his friends at school that he was constantly getting sent home.

His temper was disruptive to the class and hurtful to other students.

His father came up with a strategy to try to deter the boy from getting angry so easily. He gave his son a hammer and some nails and told him to hammer a nail into the family's fence every time the boy got angry in the future.

The following day, the boy got angry 37 times and had to hammer as many nails into the fence.

Over the next few weeks, the boy got tired of hammering nails into the fence and he gradually started to control his temper. Slowly, the number of nails he was hammering into the fence started to decrease. The boy realized that it was easier to remain calm when he started to feel angry than to gather the tools, go outside and start hammering.

Eventually, the boy stopped losing his temper altogether. His father noticed this change and told the boy to remove a nail from the fence every day that he was able to keep his temper under control.

Eventually, as the weeks went by, all of the nails had been taken out of the fence. The father and son then stood in front of the broken fence, which was completely scattered with holes.

The father turned to his son and said, 'You have done well, but look at the holes in the fence. They cannot be repaired. When you get angry at other people, it leaves scars just like the holes you see in front of you. It doesn't matter if you say I'm sorry 100 times, the injury is still there.'

> *CONTROL YOUR ANGER. IT'S ONLY*
> *ONE LETTER AWAY FROM DANGER.*

Which one are you?

Once there was a girl who was complaining to her father that her life was so hard and that she didn't know how she would get through all of her struggles. She was tired, and she felt like as soon as one problem was solved, another would arise.

Being a chef, the girl's father took her into his kitchen. He boiled three pots of water that were equal in size. He placed potatoes in one pot, eggs in another and ground coffee beans in the final pot.

He let the pots sit and boil for a while, not saying anything to his daughter.

He turned the burners off after 20 minutes, removed the potatoes from the pot and put them in a bowl. He did the same with the boiled eggs. He then used a ladle to scoop out the boiled coffee and poured it into a mug. He asked his daughter, 'What do you see?'

She responded, 'Potatoes, eggs and coffee.'

Her father told her to take a closer look and touch the potatoes. After doing so, she noticed that they were soft. Her father then told her to break open an egg. She acknowledged the hard-boiled egg. Finally, he told her to take a sip of the coffee. It was rich and delicious.

After she asked her father what all of this meant, he explained that each of the three food items had just undergone the exact same hardship—20 minutes inside of boiling water.

However, each item had a different reaction.

The potato went into the water as a strong and hard item, but after being boiled, it turned soft and weak.

The egg was fragile when it entered the water, with a thin outer shell protecting a liquid interior. However, after it was left to boil, the inside of the egg became firm and strong.

Finally, the ground coffee beans were different. Upon being exposed to boiling water, they changed the water to create something new altogether.

He then asked his daughter, 'Which are you? When you face adversity, do you respond by becoming soft and weak? Do you build strength? Or do you change the situation?'

The way you react is repeated thousands of times and becomes a routine for you. You are conditioned to be a certain way and that is a challenge. It is time to make different choices.

If you're proactive, you focus on preparing. If you're reactive, you end up on focussing on repairing.

—JOHN C. MAXWELL

Education begins from kindergarten to middle school to high school and to higher education, but when it comes to holistic learning, the application of all this is possible through the tools of skills. A skill is a learned ability to act with good execution within a given amount of time. One of the essential skills are basically good communication skills. Knowledge tells us 'what to do', skills tell us 'how to do'. The essential skills that need to be honed are listening, speaking, creativity and teamwork.

Critical thinking leads to problem solving. Teamwork leads to collaboration. Oral and written communication formulate leadership and connectivity with people. The globe has a collage of people from different ethnic groups, races and genders. We need to build rainbow bridges between different people.

Think of the possible slip-ups in any dialogue:

1. What you mean to say
2. What you actually say
3. What the other person hears
4. What they think they hear
5. What they want to say in response
6. What they do say in response
7. What you think they say, and so on.

Some of the pitfalls of speaking are caused when there is a difference between appearance and delivery. Interruptions and pretending, distractions and dishonesty could be a negative.

It takes a great man to be a good listener.

—CALVIN COOLIDGE

HOW TO BE A GOOD LISTENER

- Being a good listener can help you to see the world through the eyes of others.
- It enriches your understanding and expands your capacity for empathy.
- It also increases your contact with the outside world by helping your communication skills.
- Good listening skills can provide you with a deeper level of understanding.

Listening is not the same as hearing

Hearing

- Sounds that you hear
- Passive process like breathing
- We do it without thinking.

Listening

- Listening is a learnt skill.
- It is an active process.
- Understanding is the goal of listening.

Discriminative listening

It is believed that we develop our listening ability at an early age. In the very womb of the mother, a baby begins to distinguish between the father's and mother's voice. One can distinguish between male, female, old and young voices; though they may not understand what is being said, the tone, mannerism and voice give some idea.

Comprehensive listening

Comprehensive listening involves understanding the message. Listener first needs appropriate vocabulary and language skills. Using overly complicated language or technical jargon, therefore, can be a barrier to comprehensive listening.

Comprehensive listening is further complicated by the fact that two different people listening to the same thing may understand the message in two different ways. This problem can be multiplied in a group setting, like a classroom.

Verbal signals can greatly aid communication and comprehension.

The three types of listening in inter-personal relationships are ICT, which stands for Informational, Critical, Therapeutic listening:

1. Informational Listening (Listening to learn)
2. Critical listening (Listening to evaluate and analyse)
3. Therapeutic or Empathetic Listening (Listening to understand feelings and emotions)

In reality, you may have more than one goal for listening at any given time. For example, you may be listening to learn whilst also attempting to be empathetic. EMPATHY is the ability to understand and share the feelings of another.

1. Informational listening

Whenever you listen to learn something, you are engaged in informational listening.

This is true in many day-to-day situations, in education and at work, when you listen to the news, watch a documentary, when a friend tells you a recipe, or when you are talked through a technical problem in a computer. Like these, there are many other examples of informational listening.

Informational listening, especially in formal settings like in work meetings or in education set-ups, is often accompanied by note-taking, which is a way of recording key information, so that it can be reviewed later.

2. Critical listening

We can be said to be engaged in critical listening when the goal is to evaluate or scrutinize what is being said. Critical listening is a much more active behaviour than informational listening and usually involves some sort of problem-solving or decision-making.

Critical listening is akin to critical reading; both involve analysis of the information being received and alignment with what we already know or believe.

While informational listening may be mostly concerned with receiving facts and/or new information, critical listening is about analysing opinions and making a judgement.

When the word 'critical' is used to describe listening, reading or thinking, it does not necessarily mean that you are claiming that the information you are listening to is somehow faulty or flawed. Rather, critical listening means engaging in what you are listening to by asking yourself questions such as 'What is the speaker trying to say?' or 'What is the main argument being presented?' or 'How does what I'm hearing differ from my beliefs, knowledge and opinions?' Critical listening is, therefore, fundamental to true learning.

It is often important, when listening critically, to have an open mind and to not be biased by stereotypes or preconceived ideas. By doing this, you will become a better listener and broaden your knowledge and perception of other people and your relationships.

3. Therapeutic or empathic listening

Empathic listening involves the attempt to understand the feelings and emotions of the speaker, to put yourself into the speaker's shoes and to share their thoughts.

Empathy is not the same as sympathy; it involves more than being compassionate or feeling sorry for somebody else. It involves a deeper connection, a realization and understanding of another person's point of view.

This type of listening does not involve making judgements or offering advice but gently encouraging the speaker to explain and elaborate on their feelings and emotions.

Listening with an open mind

- Place yourself in the other person's shoes. It's easy to get lost in yourself and only consider the impact of other person's telling on you.
- Avoid comparing a person's experiences with your own.
- Avoid saying 'I' or 'me' a lot.
- Don't try to help immediately.
- Sympathize.
- Follow up.
- Know what not to do—don't interrupt when the other person is trying to make a point.
- Be silent at first.
- Reassure the person of your confidentiality.
- Be encouraging when you do speak.
- Ask meaningful and empowering questions.
- Wait for the person to open up.
- Do not interrupt with what you feel or think about the 'telling'.
- Reassure the speaker.
- When giving advice remember to make it neutral.
- Make eye contact.
- Give the speaker your full attention.
- Encourage the speaker with body language.

Double-check listening

There are three aspects to confirm the result of good listening—LRQ:

1. Listen carefully.
2. Restate.
3. Question.

If somebody asks for a particular item to be brought from the market, you have to follow this formula so that a mistake is not committed: Listen, question, restate.

• Eye contact

What is appropriate here differs from culture to culture, but establish contact with the speaker with your eyes. To not look at the other person is a way of manifesting a lack of interest. Conversely, as written in an Urdu ghazal: Love and affection can be better expressed by the eyes than by words.

• Posture

While there is no dictionary of body language, many factors like culture, relationship and situation suggest that we do speak with our bodies. If we sit leaning slightly forward, it is a sign of interest and encourages the speaker to let their thoughts and expressions flow. On the other hand, if we lean back away from the speaker, it often expresses disinterest.

• Gestures

Natural gestures as you listen can increase the speaker's sense of being heard and accepted.

• Paraphrasing

Paraphrasing is restating the speaker's thought but in fewer words. It adds nothing new, changes no directions and asks no question but summarizes the speaker's thought or feelings and informs how they have been understood.

READING SKILLS

Reading is a skill that trains us 'how' to read rather than 'what' to read. A person is known by the books that he reads. The distinction between a rich man and a poor man (in the intellectual sense) is subtle and different. A poor man has a huge television and a small library; a rich man has a huge library and a small television. The three R's of reading are plain and simple: Read, Record and Recall.

What is reading?

'Reading' is the means of looking at a series of written symbols and getting meaning from them. When we read, we use our eyes to receive written symbols (letters, punctuation marks and spaces)—a physical activity. It is also a cerebral activity—we use our brain to convert these written symbols into words, sentences and paragraphs that communicate something to us. Reading can be silent (in our head) or loud (so that other people can hear).

Reading is a receptive skill—we receive information through it. But the art of reading also requires the skill of speaking, so that we can pronounce the words that we read. Thus, reading is also a productive skill; we are both receiving information and transmitting it.

- Readers can be divided into two classes—those who read to remember and those who read to forget.
- There are worse crimes than burning books. One of them is not reading them.
- You know you've read a good book when you turn to the last page and feel as if you have lost a friend.
- 'In a good book, the best is between the lines.'—A popular Swedish proverb.
- 'Some books leave us free and some books make us free.'—Ralph Waldo Emerson.

A word of precaution

A classic cannot be re-written; it can only be re-read. A bestseller is the gilded tomb of a mediocre writer.

Reading parameters

- There is no substitute for reading a book.
- Book lovers habitually accumulate more than they can actually read. One usually confuses the purchase of books with the acquisition of their contents.
- Arguments over whether it's better to read, say, Dante's *Inferno* or Dan Brown's *Inferno* will always remain.
- There is a plethora of free ebooks; pick and choose what to read.
- The old 'no talking' signs in libraries were there for a reason. It's not what we read but how we read it that matters.
- Reading is a broad church. But it is still a church. It might behove the congregation to bow its head occasionally in silent contemplation.

The people who read are the people who lead

See the groups at railway bookstalls, the crowds in the bookstores, the large number of young people in the libraries of Kolkata and Chennai. More and more people are reading. Here are a few points to consider:

- The question for more and more people in today's world is not 'can you read?' but 'can you read well?'
- Reading walks hand-in-hand with freedom. Those in bondage are not given books. The more we read, the freer we are. Reading opens the doors to possibilities, alternatives and options that we could not see before.
- Read what Skimmer calls 'the literature of dignity.' The great prose and poetry of your culture and others that depict characters struggling to free themselves from persons and situations that seek to diminish their personal worth.
- Read for at least half-an-hour every day. If the average reader reads for 30 minutes a day, he can read 40 books in a year—a great education.
- Be selective. Four centuries ago, 1,000 books were published in a year; today, a 1,000 books are published in a day. Some are trash; others, unforgettable experiences. You don't feed rubbish to your body. Don't feed it to your mind.
- Be critical when you read. Reading is thinking with questions. What's the author saying? Do I agree with him? Is his reasoning sound? Give the author your eyes but not your mind.
- Talk about your reading. This forces you to digest what

you have read and enriches you with another person's reactions.
- And, above all, remember: A bestseller is the gilded tomb of a mediocre writer.

SPEAKING SKILLS

SPEAKING SKILLS...WHY DO WE NEED THEM? Both written and verbal communication skills are of utmost importance for they set the tone for how people perceive you.

One of the common fears among people is to stand up and speak. Fear is actually the adrenaline in a person to be an effective speaker. It is the desire to communicate effectively. Winston Churchill, a landmark speaker of his times, was once asked by a journalist why he sweated a lot at the podium while he was addressing the public. Was it fear? Churchill rightly retorted: 'This is the sweat of perfection!'

I keep six honest serving men, they taught me all I knew; Their names are What and Why and When, And How and Where and Who.

—RUDYARD KIPLING

WHAT and WHY: Deciding the objective

General objective

Fall into one category

- To persuade or sell
- To teach
- To stimulate thought

- To inform
- To entertain

Whatever be your general objective, there is always a need to try and ENTERTAIN your audience.

Specific objective

The specific objective will depend on the subject matter entirely.

This does not mean cracking jokes. It means that the material must be put in such a way that it is interesting and people want to listen.

Note

It is an excellent idea to write down the objective of the speech in one sentence. This has various benefits:

- It clears the speaker's minds right at the start.
- When your notes are complete, you can check that you are meeting your original aim.

WHO: Researching the audience

Audience—most important people in the whole exercise.

- What should you know about them?
- How many of them are there?
- Why are they there—are they there of their own free will? Were they sent to listen? Are they paying?
- What is their present knowledge of the subject of the talk?
- Are they likely to have any bias towards or against the subject or speaker?
- What are their expectations from the talk and the speaker?
- What is their age range and sex?

The bottom line is **Response-ability.**

Pitch your speech at the right level

A woman talking to a group of men about women's equality will be different from her talking to a group of women about it. Similarly, a computer expert talking to experts and novices will be different.

WHERE: Preparing the environment

It is important to consider where the talk is going to take place.
Practising—size of room aligned with volume of voice.

HOW: How things in the room work

- Distractions—become aware of any likely distraction for you and your audience.
- Possibility of noise/general interruption

WHEN: Timing

- Time of the day—the time after lunch is known as the 'graveyard session' in training circles.
- How long have we got—stick to the time limit.
- Right amount of material for the talk—if there is no clock in the room, take your watch off and put it on a table.

Remember, the key to speaking is based on what may be termed ABC: Accuracy, Brevity and Conciseness.

The first and last commandment of effective speaking is what may be termed: 'TALK LESS, SAY MORE'. In public speaking, one has to follow the sacrosanct three-S-system: 'STAND UP, SPEAK UP, SHUT UP.'

WRITING SKILLS

MULTUM IN PARVO: **Much in Less**

You can write but can you write well? A good writer is like a sculptor. They continually use less and less to express more and more. A sculptor takes a mound of clay as the medium and cuts away to get form and beauty. Similarly, a good writer cuts away useless words and makes every word count. In writing, as in all art, the canon is *'multum in parvo'*—less is more. 'Only the hand that erases can write the true thing.' Correct sentences are written; good sentences are often re-written.

Here are **Dos** and **Don'ts** for effective writing: Be simple. Have clarity. Brevity is the soul of wit. Let us use our words in the way we spend our money. Learning to write is learning to think.

1. Try to use picture words rather than abstract words, e.g., 'bus,' 'car,' or 'train' rather than 'vehicle,' a 'cat,' or a 'dog' rather than an 'animal.'
2. Write less, say more: Use one-syllable words rather than two-syllable words, two-syllable words rather than three, etc. For example, 'blood, tears, sweat, toil' rather than 'sacrifice, sorrow, perspiration, effort'. Why write 'subsequently', write 'later'. No more than 25 per cent of your words should have more than two syllables. Prefer vivid pictures to abstract words.
3. Use the active voice rather than the passive (not: 'The bicycle was fixed by me,' but: 'I fixed the bicycle'). Write as you talk.
4. Verbs words that denote action in every sentence.

Choose strong graphic verbs, e.g., 'Shahrukh *struggled* with the problem for days.' If you choose an effective verb, then an adverb is not needed.

5. Each word counts. Don't use two words where one can do the needful.
6. Sentences should generally be less than 18 words; vary their length as a good bowler varies his length. Keep clauses short. Eighteen is the danger alarm!
7. One paragraph, one idea. Clear writing comes from clear thinking. You don't know anything clearly, unless you can state it in writing.
8. Relate the experience of your audience; e.g., for computer buffs, your writing should be full of hardware, software, data entry, input and output, etc.
9. Write not to **impress** but to **express.**
10. The reader loses interest quickly. To hold his/her attention, be as personal as the situation allows, by using personal pronouns (I, you, she, etc.), posing questions to the reader, and using exclamation. Involve the reader to be with you within the lines and even read between the lines.
11. Writing is hard work; exert yourself. 'I think, therefore I am,' said Descartes. Indeed, writing is a form of therapy. Good sentences are not written, they are simply re-written.
12. Words move, music moves. Every language has its own music. Read your work aloud to see whether it has the correct 'feel'. Sound does come before sense, as we know from our kindergarten days.

Writing, to me, is simply thinking through my fingers.

—ISAAC ASIMOV

ADAPTABILITY

Adaptability skills define our capacity to change action and course of ways to deal with things to suit another circumstance.

> *BE WILLING TO CHANGE, BECAUSE*
> *LIFE WON'T STAY THE SAME.*

Life is neither static nor unchanging. Any species unable to adapt is doomed. Adaptability expands your capacity to handle change. It is a skill of being flexible and being able to change in order to become successful. The world will forever be different and we will have to be prepared to adapt to change. We have to be aware of changes in our environment. We also need to develop a growth mindset. Adaptability is crucial for success in today's ever-changing workplace.

LEADERSHIP SKILLS

The essence of leadership skills is decisiveness, critical thinking and team building. Valuable leadership skills include the ability to delegate, inspire and communicate effectively. They are at the core of relationship building.

Leadership skills are the strengths and abilities of individuals to demonstrate qualities that help them in the achievement of their goals.

*A leader is one who knows the way,
goes the way, and shows the way.*

—JOHN C. MAXWELL

Leadership means different things to different people around the world, and different things in different situations.

*Leaders are people who do the right thing;
managers are people who do things right.*

—WARREN BENNIS

Leaders help themselves and others do the right things. They set direction, build an inspiring vision and create something new. Leadership is about mapping out where you need to go to win as a team or an organization; and is dynamic, exciting and inspiring.

Yet, while leaders set the direction, they must also use management skills to guide their people to the right destination in a smooth and efficient way.

Leaders create an inspiring vision of the future. They motivate and inspire people to engage with that vision. They coach and build a team, so that it is more effective at achieving the vision.

Leadership is the ability to:

- Motivate
- Inspire
- Engage
- Energize
- Move people into action
- Move people into accessing their own power to make a change

Leaders can do this because they are respected. To be respected, you must be respectful. Leaders serve as a source of inspiration, courage and clarity; they tend to have a vision of what could be; they tend to have a strong character or personality, which may or may not be charismatic. Leaders tend to be disciplined; they do not abuse their power or authority. Leaders make strategic decisions that will shape conflict.

10 skills for living a good life

1. Never put off till tomorrow what you can do today.
2. Never trouble another for what you can do yourself.
3. Never spend your money before you have it.
4. Never buy what you do not want because it is cheap; it will never be dear to you.
5. Pride costs us more than hunger, thirst, and cold.
6. Never repent of having eaten too little.
7. Nothing is troublesome that we do willingly.
8. Don't let the evils which have never happened cost you pain.
9. Always take things by their smooth handle.
10. When angry, count to 10 before you speak; if very angry, count to 100.[3]

Things turn out best for the people who make the best of the way things turn out.

—JOHN WODEN

---

[3]'Jeffersonian Minimalism: Thomas Jefferson's 10 Rules for a Good Life', *The Minimalists*, https://www.theminimalists.com/jefferson/. Accessed on 30 April, 2023.

4

CHARACTER BUILDING

Private victories precede public victories. You can't invert that process any more than you can harvest a crop before you plant it.

Private victories precede public victories. You cannot invert that process any more than you can harvest a crop before you plant it.

—STEPHEN COVEY

The word 'character' comes from the Greek language, meaning 'to make a mark'. Your character is your mark on the world. Trustworthiness, respect, responsibility, fairness, a caring attitude and citizenship are the hallmarks of character.

Character counts. An essential factor to success is character.

Success is always temporary. When all is said and done, the only thing you have left is your character.

—VINCE GILL

Indeed, with character, you will, to the best of your ability, say and do what is right. A true commitment is a promise to yourself. Economic success is built on moral foundations—faith, discipline and contracts. The two are integral to success—creation of wealth and the cultivation of character.

Character is a composite of habit. Habits are like cables that get intertwined in the passage of time that cannot be broken.

Three in one: First, what others think you are; secondly, what you think you are and finally, the person you really are!

Complete your own work on time, be neat and punctual, and always show respect for others.

The leitmotif of character-building is helping to make someone emotionally stronger, more independent and better at dealing with problems.

One must be humble; humility is the beginning of wisdom.

One must live following one's principles and values. You must practise self-discipline, and, above all, be accountable.

HERE COMES A FACT CHECK

1. How I look is not as important as how I act.
2. I treat others the way I want them to treat me.
3. I am a good sport; I follow the rules, take turns and play fair.
4. It is okay to laugh at funny things, but not to laugh at others.
5. I do not gossip.
6. When I am sad, I help myself feel better by thinking of things that are good in my life.
7. In order to have friends, I must act in a kind way.

8. I believe that I am someone who can do important things.
9. 'What I say' and 'how I say it' tells others the kind of person I am.
10. I appreciate my family, teachers and school.
11. I treat everyone with respect.
12. When I listen, I show others that I care about them.
13. I am being a good citizen when I volunteer to help others.
14. I think for myself and make smart choices that are good for me.
15. Each day offers a new start to do my best.
16. I try to understand what my friends are feeling.
17. Everyone makes mistakes, so instead of getting angry at myself, I try to do better.
18. I do not give up; I keep trying until I can do my work.
19. Sharing with others makes me feel good and makes them feel good, too.
20. I work out my problems without hurting myself or others.
21. I am being polite when I wait for my turn and say 'please' and 'thank you'.
22. When I smile at people, they usually smile back.
23. I encourage my friends to do their best.
24. My values guide me to do what is right.
25. I am honest; I do not cheat or steal.
26. When I am angry, I use self-control and do not hurt others. I count to 100 before reacting.
27. I am being creative when I dance, draw, paint or write a poem or story.
28. When I do what I say I will do, I am being responsible.
29. I am grateful for what I have, so I share it with others.
30. I try to learn something new each day.

31. When things do not go my way, I stop and think of what I can do to make them better.
32. I do not make fun of other people because I don't know what their life is like.
33. I feel successful when I do my best.
34. Everyone has good and bad feelings.
35. I am being punctual when I am on time and do not keep people waiting.
36. When I cooperate with others, I get more done.
37. I follow the rules and try to make my school/workplace a better place.
38. I like to get to know people who are different from me.
39. Since I tell the truth, my friends trust me.
40. I look for what is good in others and I say what I like about them.
41. I buy only what I need and save my money.
42. When I use my time wisely, there is usually enough time to do what I want to do.
43. I think before I act; how I act affects how others treat me.
44. Using manners helps me keep my friends.
45. I have courage to stand up for people who are teased.
46. Before I do something, I ask myself, 'Is it safe?'
47. I am me. I do not try to be like someone else.
48. I care about living things on Earth, so I recycle and do not litter.
49. When I write down what I think and feel, I learn more about myself.
50. I plan ahead and think about what I want to do when I grow up.

*Character builds slowly but it can be torn
down with incredible swiftness.*

—FAITH BALDWIN

Character building requires effort or endurance to a degree that it strengthens or improves a person's character. This helps to make a person emotionally stronger, more independent and better at dealing with problems.

Knowledge will give you power, but character, respect.

—BRUCE LEE

There are essentially two skills for character building—self-awareness and self-respect. Good character of a person builds over time.

5 ways to develop your character:

1. Do what you say you will do.
2. Take responsibility for your decisions.
3. Know your boundaries and boundaries of others.
4. Understand your strengths.
5. Learn to distinguish between your own needs and wants.

Character is the link between who you actually are and who people expect you to be.

The greatest architecture is building character.

—LEWIS F. KORNS

CAUTION

Never judge a person by a past or present situation; judge a person by the character he has built along the way.

Although this popular saying may sound hackneyed, it is true:

'When wealth is lost, nothing is lost;

When health is lost, something is lost;

When character is lost, all is lost.'

The bottom line is: Be more concerned about your character than your reputation. It is character that will strengthen you. The greatest glory in living lies not in never falling but in rising every time we fall.

TRYING IS BETTER THAN CRYING.

Being faithful in the smallest things is the way to gain, maintain and demonstrate the strength needed to accomplish something.

MORAL CHARACTER IS THE DNA
OF SUCCESS AND HAPPINESS.

Character building implies an effort that builds or improves upon an individual's mental and moral characteristics.

Discipline ↓	Character building implies some degree of discipline whereby an individual makes sacrifices and hardships to solve a problem or achieve a goal. Beyond any knowledge, we gain from experience. We can transform our capacity to focus and direct our efforts towards a purpose even if we aren't feeling particularly motivated.
Comradery ↓	The experience of working towards common goals as a team in an environment of competition and constraints.
Accountability and Responsibility ↓	The experience of being trusted with accountability or responsibility for something of importance—we are given roles in helping and serving as a good example.
Risk-taking ↓	Calculated risk-taking is a fundamental aspect of character-building. Risk surrounds all things in life and can be managed by the way we build life skills and resilience
Leadership ↓	The experience of leading others towards a common purpose. For example, leadership roles in a sports team, such as a captain of a cricket team.
Debate ↓	The experience of arguing and trying to persuade others. It builds admirable character traits, such as tolerance for disagreement and personal resilience.

Honour	An honour system is a system of rules and values that is implemented by placing trust in the members of a group as opposed to monitoring and control. This is critical to character-building, as individuals who are tightly controlled never have an opportunity to prove that they are worthy of trust and may become resentful of values where there was potential to take pride in them. For example, a school shop without a cashier or monitoring system whereby students are trusted to leave payment. This requires the school to build a culture that values both trust and honour.
Freedom	Character building implies vivid experiences whereby individuals make mistakes, fail or succeed with their own efforts. This requires freedom.
Personal reflection	Beyond the dramatic aspects of character building such as risk-taking, periods of quiet, personal reflection also build character. For example, the practice of walking or sitting quietly in nature and emptying one's mind of compulsive thoughts.
Goals	The experience of setting and working towards a goal. For example, an athlete who trains each day with a goal to improve their performances.

Failure — The experience of failing despite one's best efforts. For example, an individual who takes on overly ambitious and optimistic goals may appear to fail but may have great value in developing knowledge and elusive traits such as persistence and resilience.

Overcoming fears — Activities that people commonly fear or find difficult tend to be character building. For instance, the process of mastering public speaking is character building.

Culture — Emersion in the values, norms, expectations, language, symbol, history, tradition, past art, fiction, myths, folklore and entertainment of cultures can build character. For example, participating in a local festival or reading a great work of literature. This provides a framework for understanding the world and interacting with others in a positive way.

Doing good — Selfless acts are character building as are structured activities that do good without reward, such as volunteering.

Improve — Improvization is an activity that shakes people out of behaviour patterns to such an extent that it may be character building. Improvization builds character traits such as flexibility, adaptability and capacity to cooperate.

Toil — Toil is work that is manual and intense. The process of devoting your full attention to humble work can be character building.

Character building generally requires a focus on several character strengths such as zest, grip, curiosity, optimism, self-control, gratitude and social intelligence. It requires many social skills—one must listen to others, follow the steps, follow the rules, ignore distractions, stay calm with others and do nice things for others. The essence of character in life requires courage and fortitude. It involves a comprehensive approach that includes a robust curriculum. Good character and education can provide ground rules for life for adults and young people. What is needed is an educational system that is truly man-making.

Character is the real foundation of all worthwhile success.

—JOHN HAYS HAMMOND

Self-image is primary to success. Believe in the first and last commandment—no one on the face of the earth can make you feel inferior without your permission. No one will ever sponsor a person who looks down on themselves. Character to build a self-image is a must for development. One cannot be respected unless one respects himself/herself. The mirror image is not a mirage—it reflects what is within and what is without. It is a reciprocal process—if we can respect ourselves, we will respect others.

The choice is yours—what people want to look like on the outside depends on what is actually within everyone in this world. Believe in the maxim that nobody on the face of the earth can make you feel inferior without your permission. Success is easy once you believe in yourself. This depends on the fodder that you have built over the years with your character development.

Artificial Intelligence (AI) is the theory and development of computer systems which are able to perform tasks normally requiring human intelligence, such as visual perception, speech recognition, decision-making and translation between languages. Machines are digital, whereas the human brain is analogous. Human intelligence is based on the variants humans encounter in life and responses they get, which may result in millions of functions overall in their lives. Machines can mimic human behaviour and perform human-like actions. The essence of human behaviour is character. The essence of character is living a life of courage and fortitude each day that ensures alignment of your character and reputation. It takes positive attitude and effort to build character.

Four aspects of character

- Moral character: The qualities that help us be our best self, including trustworthiness, respect, responsibility, fairness, a caring attitude and citizenship.
- Performance character: Getting to the top is important but what is more important is the way we choose to get there.
- Intellectual character: Cheap literature can belittle us in our own eyes. Good literature kindles the imagination; cheap literature satisfies the imagination.
- Civic character: It is not our inner world but the outer world that matters the most. It is fulfiling our civic responsibility that will make the world a better place. Freedom is good

if we remember the maxim: My freedom ends where your nose begins!

Character-building skills

Character traits like autonomy, curiosity, resourcefulness and reflection are the skills to hone. These characteristics centre around ethics. This might encompass traits like honesty, integrity, compassion and respect.

Civic virtues make someone a contributing member of society.

Train yourself with interpersonal skills that offer emotional, social and intellectual tools needed to achieve success on a personal level, an interpersonal level and within your community and workplaces.

What are examples of character building?

Character building

Character building implies some degree of discipline whereby an individual makes sacrifices and faces hardship to solve a problem or achieve a goal.

You have to descend into the depths of humility to climb the heights of character.

The crux of our character often comes to a test at moments of moral crisis. In Lewis Carroll's *Through the Looking Glass*, Alice had to become small to enter wonderland.

Our character is based on our habits. Habits have a great gravity pull. They will pull you down during character building.

The essence of character lies in your strengths, skills and habits.

Without character, you cannot be trusted; and if you cannot be trusted, you cannot lead.

5

SELF-IMAGE

What do you think you look like? Self-image is how you perceive yourself. It is the number of self-impressions that we have built up overtime. You see your personality: what kind of a person do you think you are is the key associated with self-image. Improving your self-image can be done through introspection.

Self-image is important because how we think about ourselves affects how we feel about ourselves and how we interact with others and the world around us. Positive self-image can boost our physical, mental, emotional and spiritual well-being.

There are four types of self-image:

1. How you see yourself.
2. How others see you.
3. How you perceive others see you.
4. How you perceive you see yourself.

Four characteristics of a healthy self-image:

1. It makes you feel confident.
2. It makes you compare yourself to others in a positive way.
3. It makes you content in how you look at yourself and believe in your own abilities.
4. Finally, positive feedback received from friends and family on looks and abilities empowers you.

How can I improve my self-esteem?

1. Please be kind to yourself.
2. Try to recognize positives.
3. Build a support network.
4. Try talking therapy.
5. Set yourself a challenge.
6. Finally, look after yourself.

We need to create a positive self-image. It is something a person cultivates as a result of what life teaches him; it can reflect your real self to the outside world on account of the character of a good self-image.

IF IT'S NOT WHO YOU ARE THAT HOLDS YOU BACK, IT'S WHO YOU THINK YOU ARE NOT.

Having a positive self-image: Good self-esteem is how you will bring in a sense of confidence in everything about you. It's a lesson no one can teach you. It depends on how one creates a positive self-image. This is not something that's fixed on a scale. Constant self-improvement from your side will boost your image. You should nurture the positives in you.

Accepting inputs will develop good self-esteem.

Change the habit of being right all the time. In our life, the same applies. 'I'm right' is not the gospel truth. Learn to accept inputs from people around you

Give space. Listening and giving space to others is a good personal trait. Self-esteem should give the same feeling to others. You should not make others feel low. We should not make other people feel that their self-respect is being tested. Give equal space to everyone.

Be humble. A super intelligent person would be right behind you. The habit of feeling 'I'm better than everyone else' will not reflect positivity over time.

Being humble does not mean being flagged. If there is a need to speak, do speak.

Extend your support when there's need for it. (Two things should not be given unless asked for: 1. Salt 2. Advice)

Learning from mistakes and improving yourself is essential in addition to having basic good traits.

Comparing yourself with others is not how you develop your self-esteem.

There is a thin line between confidence and overconfidence. Tread carefully on this path.

SELF-MOTIVATION IS THE KEY. YOU WON'T BE SUCCESSFUL WITHOUT IT.

SELF-ANALYSIS: YOUR NEED TO SEE YOURSELF

It becomes hard especially when there's room for comparison with others. Don't obsess with self-image so that you start looking good and do well. Take care of yourself; for that you need good food; go to sleep; have good friends, an active lifestyle, and a positive mind; look back. Sometimes you have to look back to see how far you made the journey projecting a self-image it will help people get a sense of their potential and capabilities.

Are you born to win or conditioned to lose? Think about it. We all are born to win, but as we grow up, the negativities that bombard us throughout our lifetime conditions us to doubt ourselves and, eventually, lose.

It is hard to give a consistent marvellous performance, if you do not see yourselves as a marvellous performer. Whether you climb the staircase to success or go down the escalator to the basement of failure, it all depends on you—how you think about yourselves.

Think about yourselves as incapable and undeserving and you will feel it. Think about yourselves as capable and deserving and you will feel it.

While delving into our self-image, we must remember that the mind turns into a reality whatever image we conjure in it about ourselves.

Imagine a 12-inch plank lying on the floor. Can you walk on it? Of course, it is safely lying on the floor. Now put the same plank between two buildings at the tenth storey. Can you still walk on it? It's a different game altogether.

Earlier, you saw yourselves walking on the plank safely. Now, you see yourselves falling off the plank between the two buildings. It creates fear. Your mind is busy converting it into reality. Result? You can't walk.

Accepting yourself

Do you accept yourself as you are? Are you happy with who you are and what you are?

If not, then change it. First, accept yourself. Your situation will start to change. Make sure it is healthy self-acceptance and not an inflated ego. In fact, a person with an inflated ego is actually a person with low self-esteem.

Education and intelligence are two different things

Henry Ford, the founder of Ford Motor Company, quit school at 14. Thomas J. Watson, the founder of the International Business Machines Corporation (IBM), was a $6 salesman initially and went on to become the chairman of the board.

Reasons for poor self-image

- Finding faults frequently
- Ridiculing a person's ability or talent. This distorts a person's self-image.
- Exaggerating a person's mistakes. For example, a girl drops a dish and the mother shouts, 'You are always breaking things. You are so clumsy.'
- Compounding the negativity by feeding it more in adult life. For example, you have a spouse who is always finding faults in you.
- Identifying a single failure as a whole and thinking you are a failure in life.
- Comparing experiences of other people with your own. This has nothing to do with capabilities. Every person grows differently as everyone has different experiences in life.
- Comparing physical features of other people with your own.

The six dimensions of a person's self-image are:

- Physical dimension: how a person evaluates his or her appearance.
- Psychological dimension: how a person evaluates his or her personality.
- Intellectual dimension: how a person evaluates his or her intelligence.
- Skills dimension: how a person evaluates his or her social and technical skills.
- Moral dimension: how a person evaluates his or her values and principles.
- Sexual dimension: how a person feels he or she fits into society's masculine/feminine norms.

A positive self-image is having a good view of yourself; for example:

- Seeing yourself as an attractive and desirable person.
- Having an image of yourself as a smart and intelligent person.
- Seeing a happy, healthy person when you look in the mirror.
- Believing that you are at least somewhat close to your ideal version of yourself.
- Thinking that others perceive you as all of the above as well as yourself.[4]

---

[4] Ackerman, Courtney E., 'What is Self-Image in Psychology? How Do We Improve it?', *PositivePsychology.com*, 22 December 2018, https://tinyurl.com/msmzpfnx. Accessed on 30 April 2023.

A negative self-image is the flipside of the above; it looks like:

- Seeing yourself as unattractive and undesirable.
- Having an image of yourself as a stupid or unintelligent person.
- Seeing an unhappy, unhealthy person when you look in the mirror.
- Believing that you are nowhere near your ideal version of yourself.
- Thinking that others perceive you as all of the above as well as yourself.

Being spotless

Jim worked at a radio station all his life. He was a well-known and famous radio show host. All of his friends and colleagues knew him by one feature: If he's on-air, he is always wearing a suit and a tie. They laughed at him: 'No one ever sees you; why do you dress like that?'

One day, Jim was invited to appear on television. There was a show dedicated to the oldest radio employees. For the first time, the people who only knew him by his voice would see him.

Before the recording of the show, the director came to Jim and asked:

'Usually you arrive on time, but today you are 10 minutes late. It's not horrible, but I'm still interested to know why?'

'You see,' Jim answered, 'at the last moment, when I was already dressed up, I noticed that I don't have new socks. For the first time, I was invited to be on TV, and I thought that simply wearing clean socks is not enough. I need to wear new socks. So, I needed to go to the store to buy a new pair of socks.'

'But why do you need new socks?' The director was surprised. 'You could have come without the socks because we will only be filming your close-up, over the waist.

Jim responded, 'You see, to be spotless on-air, I need to feel spotters too—starting with my shirt and finishing with the pen in my pocket. And if my socks have holes in them, or my shoes are dirty, I'm not spotless anymore.'

Two grains

Two grains were lying side-by-side on the fertile soil.

The first grain said: 'I want to grow up! I want to put down roots deep into the ground and sprout from the ground. I dream to blossom in delicate buds and proclaim the coming of spring. I want to feel the warm rays of sun and the dew drops on my petals!'

This grain grew up and became a beautiful flower.

The second grain said: 'I'm afraid. If I put down my roots into the ground, I don't know what they will face there. If I grow tender stems, they can be damaged by wind. If I grow flowers, they may be disrupted. So I'd rather wait for a safer time.'

Thus, the second grain kept waiting, until the chicken that passed by pecked on it.

You are what you are

One day, a king came to his garden and saw withering and dying trees, bushes and flowers.

An oak said it was dying because it couldn't be as high as a pine.

A pine tree was falling down because it could not produce grapes like a grapevine.

Meanwhile, the grapevine was dying because it couldn't blossom like a rose.

But soon, the king found a single plant with a pleasing heart, blooming and fresh.

The king asked the plant, 'All the trees and flowers here are withering, and you are flourishing. Why?'

The plant said, 'I think it comes naturally. You have planted me because it was your wish and choice. If you would like to grow an oak, grapes or rose, you would plant them. And I cannot be anything else than what I am. So I try to develop my best qualities.'

Look at yourself. You can only be yourself. It is impossible for you to become someone else. You can enjoy life and blossom or you can wither if you do not accept yourself.

The rose

In a garden filled with bushes, out from between a load of grass and weeds, there appeared, as if from nowhere, a white rose. It was as white as snow; its petals looked like velvet and the morning dew shone from its leaves like resplendent crystals. The flower couldn't see herself, so she had no idea how pretty she was. And so it was that she spent the few days left of her life, until wilting set on, without knowing that everyone around her was amazed by her and her perfection—her perfume, the softness of her petals, her elegance. She didn't realize that everyone who saw her spoke well of her. The weeds that surrounded her were fascinated by her beauty and lived in a state of enchantment at her aroma and appearance.

On a hot and sunny day, a girl was strolling through the garden, thinking about how many lovely things Mother Nature has given us, when she suddenly saw a white rose in a forgotten part of the garden. The rose was beginning to fade and wilt.

'It's been days since it rained,' she thought. 'If the rose stays here till tomorrow, it'll wither and die. I'll take it home and put it in the lovely vase that I got as a present.'

And so she did. With all her love, she put the wilting white rose in water, inside a lovely colourful glass vase, and placed it by the window.

What the young girl didn't realize was that the reflection in the window meant that, for the first time, the rose got to see herself and what she looked like.

'Is that me?' thought the rose. Little by little, her drooping leaves began to rise, once again stretching up towards the sun; and, gradually, the rose recovered her former appearance. When she was totally back to her best, she looked at her reflection and saw that she was indeed a beautiful flower. She thought, 'Wow! Till now I hadn't realized who I was. How could I have been so blind?'

THE PROCESS IS MORE IMPORTANT THAN THE RESULT.

The lion is the king of the jungle but how can he be the king of the jungle? He is not the biggest—the elephant is probably one of the biggest animals. He cannot be the fastest as that is the cheetah. He cannot be the smartest either. So, if he is not the biggest, the fastest and the smartest, how can he be the king of the jungle? His mentality!

When a lion walks up to an elephant, he thinks of lunch.

The elephant runs—it's all in the mentality.

When a male lion walks, he may be surrounded by a pack of hyenas. The hyenas may outnumber him, but the lion is still the king because of his mentality.

What happens when you don't get what you deserve?

What happens when you don't get when you get pushed for?

What happens when you get no reward?

What happens when no one is encouraging you?

What happens doesn't matter. You are a lion.

Lions love to hunt. They love the process as much as they love the prize. Some of us like to score, but we do not like the process. A true hunter's goal is not the prize; they love the process. That is why they love to hunt.

If we look within, we realize that all things are created twice. These scripts come from people, not principles.

EVERYTHING IS CREATED TWICE, FIRST IN THE MIND AND THEN IN THE PRESENT TENSE PAR EXCELLENCE.

Let us re-look at ourselves, our self-image. Let us dissolve, diffuse and dissipate in order to recreate. There is nothing like fixities and definites. The 'I AM' is always in a state of continuum.

IT'S NOT WHO YOU ARE THAT HOLDS YOU BACK.
IT'S WHO YOU THINK YOU ARE.

Now is the time to take up the mantle and proceed on the road to success!

6

MOTIVATIONAL SNIPPETS

True wit is nature to advantage dress'd.
What oft was thought, but ne'er so well express'd.

—ALEXANDER POPE

1
EMPTY YOUR CUP

A little learning is a dangerous thing; Drink deep, or taste not the
Pierian spring: There shallow draught intoxicates the brain,
And drinking largely sobers us again.

—ALEXANDER POPE

Once there was a university professor, who was known as an extremely knowledgeable person. He had done a lot of research in the field of philosophy. The professor had a keen interest in Zen Buddhism practices and wanted to learn more about them. He visited a famous Japanese Zen master to learn the pearls of Zen wisdom.

When he reached the Zen master's place, the disciples took him to the Zen master's room. The Zen master's physical appearance was affable and his spirit was lofty. His face was shimmering and lot of positive energy could be felt around him. After welcoming his visitor, the Zen master asked the professor the reason for his visit. The professor told him the motive of his visit, 'I have come to ask you to teach me about Zen Buddhism.'

The Zen master asked the professor, 'You are known for your knowledge everywhere. Please share something with me.'

The Professor started telling him about his research in different fields, one by one. After some time, he also started sharing his knowledge about Zen. The Zen master listened to him silently for an hour. The Zen master interrupted and asked the professor if he would like some tea.

Knowing he should accept, the professor smiled and thanked the Zen master for his generosity.

One of the Zen master's disciples disappeared and then quickly reappeared with two cups and some steaming hot tea.

The master started pouring the tea into the cup and smiled at the professor. The professor continued to share his knowledge on Zen Buddhism with the master. The Zen master was pouring the tea slowly-slowly and soon the cup got completely filled. But he did not stop and kept pouring the tea in the cup. The tea started overflowing onto the table. The professor noticed this and continued to watch as it overflowed. Soon, the tea started falling on the robes of professor and he could no longer restrain himself.

The professor put his hand up and exclaimed, 'Stop! Can't you see? The cup is already full. It's overflowing. No more will go in!' The Zen master did not stop and kept pouring more tea.

The professor got angry and rushed to leave. The Zen master called him back, 'Professor, please listen.' The professor did not stop. The master ran behind him and stopped him.

The Zen master calmly explained the reason why he kept pouring the tea in the cup even after it overflowed. The Zen master said, 'You are here to ask questions. Yet you come full. You have your own ideas and have no space for more. Until you have room for more, you will not accept new information. You are like that cup of tea. How can I show you Zen unless you empty your cup first?'

2
LIFE IS A CUP OF COFFEE

The container is not as important as the content. Appearance may be important, but, at the end of the day, it is reality that matters. Everything is interdependent, not absolute.

A group of best friends decided to have their alumni get-together at the residence of one of their favourite university professors. The professor was very popular among the university students and had been a mentor to many of them. They decided to make a surprise visit to the professor. All the planning was done; and on a predefined date, they visited their most popular and old university professor's house.

It was quite a happy moment for not only the professor but also for the friends (students of the professor) as some of them were meeting after a long time. Everyone was trying to know the whereabouts of and the developments in their friends' lives after leaving college. They shared with each other how they moved ahead in life. A few became good leaders, with senior positions in the corporate world; whereas, a few were doing good in the business world. All of them had gotten married and had wonderful families. Everyone had followed his/her own timing in life for achieving the milestones. There was a quality conversation going on, but somehow the conversation soon diverted to complaints about work, relationships, stress and tension in life.

The professor offered them coffee and went to kitchen to ask his wife to prepare coffee for all his students. After 10–15 minutes, his beautiful wife came out with a pleasant smile. One thing to be noticed was that she brought the coffee in different kinds of cups—crystal cups, glass cups, ceramic cups, shiny ones, some plain-looking, some ordinary, some exquisite and some expensive ones. The students thought the the professor must not have the same kind of cups and due to large number of guests, his wife had served the coffee in different cups.

When all of them had a cup in hand, the professor said, 'If you noticed, all the nice-looking and expensive cups have been taken, leaving behind the ordinary, plain and cheap ones!!!'

It was surprising moment as nobody had noticed that there were some extra cups of coffee left; and while taking their cup, nobody had taken the ordinary cups and so and all of them were left on the serving tray.

The professor continued, 'Every single one of you wanted the best cup. While it is, of course, normal for you to want only the best for yourselves, that can also be the source of much of your dissatisfaction, problems, stress and tension in life.'

All the friends were confused and looked at the professor;

they could not understand the connection between having coffee in a cup and the stress and tension of life.

The professor continued to speak and explained after seeing their curious faces, 'Be assured that the cup itself adds no quality to the coffee. In most cases, it is just more expensive; and in some cases, it even hides what we drink. What you really wanted was the coffee, not the cup! But you unconsciously went for the best cups…and then you began to eye each other's cups.'

Always remember one thing: Life is coffee and jobs, while money, status or position in society and love etc., are the cups! They are just tools to hold and contain life. The type of cup we have does not define or change the quality of the life we live. Please don't let the cups drive you! Enjoy the coffee!'

∽

3
THE RETIRING CARPENTER

In order to be sure of success in any enterprise, we must follow the carpenter's rule: 'measure twice, cut once'.

There was a highly skilled carpenter who was just about to retire. He was retiring after a long and dedicated career in building houses. He was a master at his work and was extremely famous for his extraordinary work.

At the very beginning of his career, when he joined a prominent contractor, he had been required to make a very special promise. The carpenter had to promise the contractor that every house he built would be built as if it was the most important project he had ever been given. He also had to promise that every house would be built with creativity, dedication, love and care.

Getting ready to retire, the carpenter went into his boss's office to inform him about his plans. The carpenter said, 'The house that I have just completed will be my last. I would like to retire from the service now.'

The boss said, 'I am sorry to see you leaving our organization. May I request you to be kind enough to do a final favour for me?'

The carpenter replied, 'Please, Sir, tell me, what can I do for you?'

The boss said, 'Just build one more house for me, then you're free to go.'

The carpenter, who respected his boss to a great extent, agreed and immediately started to work on the new house. But unlike every other house he had built over the past few years, he did not use the full extent of his expertise with this final one. He took every shortcut he knew to finish the project in record time. The only reason behind this decision was that he wanted to begin his second innings after retirement at the earliest. He cut corners, used inferior material and hurried to get the task over with.

Within weeks, the carpenter completed the house. And finally, the carpenter called his employer and showed him the house.

The employer was very happy and grateful to him. He said to the carpenter in a gentle tone, 'Thanks for doing this personal favour for me.'

Then, the employer handed over some papers and keys to the front door to the carpenter and said, 'These are for you. The house you just built is my parting gift for all your years of hard work and dedication.'

The carpenter was astounded. He could not believe that the home he had just built was his own. If he had known this, he would have put his very best into it!

4
KNOW THE VALUE, NOT THE PRICE

A cynic is a man who knows the price of everything and the value of nothing.

—OSCAR WILDE

At the beginning of a new school year, a class teacher stood in front of her students, holding a $100 bill.

She told them, 'Put your hands up if you want this money.'

Every hand in the room went up. The teacher said, 'I am going to give this money to someone here, but first, let me do this…'

She took the bill and crumpled it up in her hands, before asking, 'Who still wants it?'

The hands stayed up.

The teacher then dropped the bill on the floor, stomped and grinded it into the ground, and picked it back up. 'How about now?' she asked.

The hands stayed up.

'Class, I hope you see the lesson here. It didn't matter what I did to this money, you still wanted it because its value stayed the same. Even with its creases and dirtiness, it's still worth $100.'

She continued, 'It's the same with us. There will be similar times in your life when you're dropped, bruised and muddied. Yet no matter what happens, you *never* lose your value.'

5
THE TWO WOLVES

GIGO: Garbage In, Garbage Out.

An old chief sat down to teach his grandson about life.

'There's a fight going on inside me,' he told the young boy, '…a fight between two wolves. One wolf is evil. It's full of malice, anger, greed, self-pity and false pride. The other is good. It's full of peace, love, joy, kindness and humility. The same fight is going on inside you and everyone else on the face of the earth.'

The grandson was quiet, pondering this revelation for a moment, before asking, 'Grandfather, which wolf will win?'

The old man smiled and replied, 'The one you feed.'

6
BREAD AND BUTTER

As you sow so, you reap. What you put in, comes out.
The scale of life is always balanced.

A long time ago, a baker and a farmer lived in the same small English village.

These two men had a friendly arrangement in place, in which the farmer would sell a pound of butter to the baker each day.

One morning, the baker decided to weigh the butter to see if he'd received the correct amount. To his surprise, he discovered that the farmer had sold him less butter than he had paid for.

Angry about the unfairness, he took the farmer to court.

At the hearing, the judge asked the farmer whether he used any measure to weigh the butter.

'Your honour, I am but a lowly farmer and do not own a proper measure. I simply use an old-fashioned scale,' he replied.

'How do you weight the butter then?' The judge inquired.

To this, the farmer answered: 'Your honour, long before the baker started buying butter from my farm, I've been buying a pound loaf of bread from him. When he brings me the bread everyday, I place it on my scale and give him the same weight in butter. If anyone is to be blamed, it's the baker.'

7
THE BALLOONS

The secret to success is not competition.
It is sharing that will get you there.

There was once a group of 100 people attending a seminar on personal development.

In the middle of their talk, the speaker stops and decides to run an impromptu group activity. He hands out a balloon to each attendee and tells them to write their name on it.

The balloons are then collected and placed in an adjacent room.

The speaker then instructs the 100 attendees to enter that room and, within five minutes, find the balloon with their name on it.

Pandemonium breaks loose as they charge in, pushing and colliding with each other as they desperately search for their name.

The five minutes pass and nobody succeeds.

The speaker then tells each person to pick up a random balloon and give it to the person whose name is written on it. Within a few minutes, everyone has their balloon back.

8
SHARPENING YOUR AXE

Hard work is not enough; proper application is what matters.

Two lumberjacks with equal skill, experience and stature work side-by-side, chopping down trees together every single day.

However, one lumberjack works non-stop, without taking a break, whereas the other takes an hour-long lunch break every afternoon.

Despite working for less time, both lumberjacks inevitably chop the same number of trees by the end of each working day.

Puzzled and frustrated, the lumberjack who works all day long asks the other lumberjack how he manages to chop just as much as him while still taking a break.

To this, he responds: 'It's simple. I spend that one hour at home, sharpening my axe!'

9
THE CAMELS

Life seems to be a rat race; but in the race,
one should not become the rat.

A mother camel and her baby were lying down, soaking up the sun.

The baby camel asked his mother, 'Why do we have these big humps on our back?'

The mother stopped to think and then said, 'We live in the desert where there is not much water available. Our humps store water to help us survive long journeys.'

The baby camel then stopped to think and asked, 'Well, why do we have long legs with rounded feet?'

His mother replied, 'They are meant to help us walk on sand.'

The baby asked a third question, 'Why are my eyelashes so long?'

The mother replied, 'Your long eyelashes offer you protection from sand when it blows in the wind.'

Finally, the baby said, 'If all of these natural abilities have been given to us to walk through the desert, what's the use for camels in zoos?'

10
ROCKS IN THE BUCKET

Life does not cease to be funny when people die any more than it ceases to be serious when people laugh.

—GEORGE BERNARD SHAW

A lecturer at a university was giving a pre-exam lecture on time management. On his desk were a bag of sand, a bag of pebbles, some big rocks and a bucket. He asked for a volunteer to put all three grades of stone into the bucket; and a keen student duly stepped up to carry out the task, starting with the sand, then the pebbles, then the rocks, which did not fit into the bucket.

'This an analogy of poor time management,' says the lecturer, 'If you'd have put the rocks in first, then the pebbles, then the sand, all three would have fit. This is much like time management, as by completing your biggest tasks first, you leave room to complete your medium tasks and then your smaller ones. By completing your smallest tasks first, you spend so much time on them that you leave yourself unable to complete either medium of large tasks satisfactorily. Let me show you...'

And the lecturer filled the bucket again, with big rocks first, then pebbles, then sand, shaking the bucket between each step so that everything fit.

'But, Sir,' said one student, slouched at the back of the theatre, 'You've forgotten one thing...'

And the student approached the bucket, produced a can of lager, opened it and poured into the bucket. 'No matter how busy you are,' quipped the student, with a smile, 'There's always time for a quick beer!'

11
THE BUTTERFLY

Anyone that truly cares about you will never put you last on the list. You would be a priority for life.

A man found the cocoon of a butterfly. One day, a small opening appeared in the cocoon. He sat and watched the butterfly for several hours as it struggled to force its body out through the little hole. Then, it seemed to stop making any progress. It appeared to be stuck.

The man decided to help the butterfly; and with a pair of scissors, he cut open the cocoon. The butterfly emerged easily. But, something was strange. The butterfly had a swollen body and shrivelled wings. The man watched the butterfly closely, expecting it to take on its correct proportions. But nothing changed.

The butterfly stayed the same. It was never able to fly. In his kindness and haste, the man did not realize that the butterfly's struggle to get out through the small opening of the cocoon is nature's way of forcing fluid from the body of the butterfly into its wings, so that it would be ready for flight.

12
THE MONK AND THE TRAVELLERS

If there is no struggle, there is no progress.

—FREDERICK DOUGLASS

One day, a traveller was walking along a road on his journey from one village to another. As he walked, he noticed a monk tending to the ground in the fields beside the road. The monk said 'Good day' to the traveller, and the traveller nodded at the monk. The traveller then turned to the monk and said, 'Excuse me, do you mind if I ask you a question?'

'Not at all,' the monk replied.

'I am travelling from the village in the mountains to the village in the valley, and I was wondering if you knew what it is like in the village in the valley?'

'Tell me,' said the monk, 'What was your experience of the village in the mountains?'

'Dreadful!' replied the traveller, 'To be honest, I am glad to get away from there. I found the people most unwelcoming. When I first arrived, I was greeted coldly. I was never made to feel like I was a part of the village, no matter how hard I tried. The villagers keep very much to themselves; they don't take kindly to strangers. So, tell me, what can I expect from the village in the valley?'

'I am sorry to tell you,' said the monk, 'but I think your experience will be the same there.'

The traveller hung his head despondently and walked on.

A while later, another traveller who was journeying down the same road and he also came upon the monk.

'I'm going to the village in the valley,' said the second traveller, 'Do you know what it is like?'

'I do,' replied the monk. 'But first, tell me, where have you come from?'

'I've come from the village in the mountains.'

'And how was that?'

'It was a wonderful experience. I would have stayed if I could but I am committed to travelling onwards. I felt as though I was a member of the family in the village. The elders gave me a lot of advice, the children laughed and joked with me and people were generally kind and generous. I am sad to have left it. It will always hold special memories for me... What is the village in the valley like?' he asked again.

'I think you will find it much the same,' replied the monk. 'Good day to you!'

'Good day and thank you,' the traveller replied, smiled and journeyed on.

13
BELIEVE IN THE IMPOSSIBLE

People only see what they are prepared to see.

—RALPH WALDO EMERSON

Every great achievement was once considered to be impossible, until someone set a goal to make it a reality.

Lewis Carroll's famous masterpiece *Through the Looking Glass* contains a story that exemplifies the need to dream the impossible dream. There is a conversation between Alice and the Queen, which goes like this:

'I can't believe that!' said Alice.

'Can't you?' the Queen said in a pitying tone. 'Try again, draw a long breath and shut your eyes.'

Alice laughed. 'There's no use trying,' she said. 'One can't believe impossible things.'

'I dare say you haven't had much practice,' said the Queen. 'When I was your age, I always did it for half-an-hour a day. Why, sometimes I've believed as many as six impossible things before breakfast.'

∞

14
THE BLUE MARBLE

When you dare to dream, many marvels can be accomplished. The trouble is, most people never start dreaming their impossible dream.

Once upon a time, a group of children were playing with marbles. There were two teams and they were competing against each other. The leaders of each team, Chong and Joey, wanted their teams to win. Before starting the game, both leaders rushed to a nearby hut wherein lived a sage. They wanted to seek his blessings to win the game. The sage was meditating and both the children knelt before him and prayed. The sage opened his eyes and said, 'You have to give something before you can get something. What do you like most, besides your parents and friends?'

Chong said, 'I have many marbles that I love. I will give

all of them to you, if you bless me in return.' So, Chong gave all the marbles to the sage.

Joey also had many marbles. But one marble was very special to him. It was a blue marble. He did not want to give it away. He quietly felt the blue marble inside his pocket and let it stay there, while he took out all the other marbles and gave them to the sage.

The sage knew what was happening, for he was no ordinary sage. Although he blessed both the children, it was Chong who received complete blessings.

15
THE HEAVENLY SCENE

The strongest position you can be in is complete surrender.
The more we share, the more we have.

A man went to heaven. There, he saw two sections. In one section, there were a sad and malnourished group of people, wailing in hunger and all negative emotions. In the other section, there was a happy and healthy group of people with peace of mind and all the positive emotions. He couldn't believe it. *How can people be sad in heaven?*

And then he realized why. During lunchtime, the table was laid out on both the sections with all kinds of delicious food, desserts, ice creams, soups, salads and what not. People came and sat down to eat. But what's this? The spoons were awfully long. They just couldn't feed themselves with those long spoons. They were struggling to eat. No one could eat a morsel.

The man then observed the other section and was astonished. The spoons were awfully long there too, but lo and behold, the people were eating happily, enjoying every morsel. Each person fed the person sitting opposite to him through the long spoon. The man, at once, knew the secret of joy and heaven—sharing and caring for fellow people.

16
SPREADING SUNSHINE

Shared joy is doubled.

There was a little girl who was playing in her garden in the lovely sunshine. Her grandmother could not come outside as she was unwell and in bed. Her room faced the north, so it could not be flooded with sunshine. The girl thought, 'My granny's missing this lovely sunshine. I must take some sunshine for her.' She dashed back inside the house and brought a bag with her. She opened the bag and sat facing the sun, filling the sunshine in her bag. Then, she zipped the bag up and rushed to where her grandma was. 'Granny, I have brought some sunshine for you. It's warm and lovely. You will feel better now,' she said excitedly. As she opened the bag, her face fell. There was no sunshine in the bag. The bag was empty and dark from the inside.

Grandma smiled and said, 'My child, I have received your sunshine. It's there in your eyes and I can feel its warmth. I need no sun when I have you here with me.' The little girl did not understand what her beloved grandmother was saying, but she was happy because she could make her grandmother happy.

A smile is the light in your window that tells others that there is a caring and sharing person inside.

17
THE JOKE

Don't complain about the things you are not willing to change. Stop complaining. Do something.

A wise man once faced a group of people who were complaining about the same issues over and over again. One day, instead of listening to their complaints, he told them a joke and everyone cracked up laughing.

Then, the man repeated the joke. A few people smiled. Finally, the man repeated the joke for the third time, but no one reacted to it.

The man smiled and said, 'You won't laugh at the same joke more than once. So what are you getting from continuing to complain about the same problem?'

18
SECRET OF SUCCESS

We don't grow when things are easy;
we grow when we face challenges.

A boy once asked a wise old man what the secret to success is.

After listening to the boy's question, the wise man told the boy to meet him at the riverside in the morning and he would be given the answer there.

In the morning, the wise man and the boy began walking towards the river. They continued on into the river, past the point of the water covering their nose and mouth. At this time, the wise man ducked the boy under the water.

As the boy struggled to get up, the wise man continued to push him further down. The boy felt a fish slip by his leg and squirmed to get up even harder. The man eventually pulled the boy's head up, so he could get air. The boy gasped as he inhaled a deep breath of air.

The wise man said, 'What were you fighting for when you were underwater?'

The boy replied, 'Air!'

The man said, 'There! You have the secret to success! When you want to gain success as much as you wanted air when you were underwater, you will obtain it. That is the only secret!'

PILAR OUTREACH FOUNDATION

Pilar Outreach Foundation, a non-profit organization, makes all efforts to provide a society of opportunities. It is committed towards empowering underprivileged communities, women and youth to lead fulfilling lives with dignity. It believes in the three Es—Educate, Empower and Enrich. Through various programmes and initiatives, the effort of this NGO is to break down barriers and empower individuals to take control of their lives. This is done by providing educational opportunities, vocational training, medical healthcare and mentorship to help underprivileged youth and women to build the skills and confidence that they need to succeed. The organization has the firm belief that together we can make a difference.

Pilar Outreach Foundation
Head office: N-32, Jangpura Extension, New Delhi 110014.
pilaroutreach@gmail.com